GAUDÍ

Introduction to his architecture

Text **Juan-Eduardo Cirlot**, photography **Pere Vivas**, **Ricard Pla**

TRIANGLE ▼ **BOOKS**

Park Güell

Cripta de la Colònia Güell

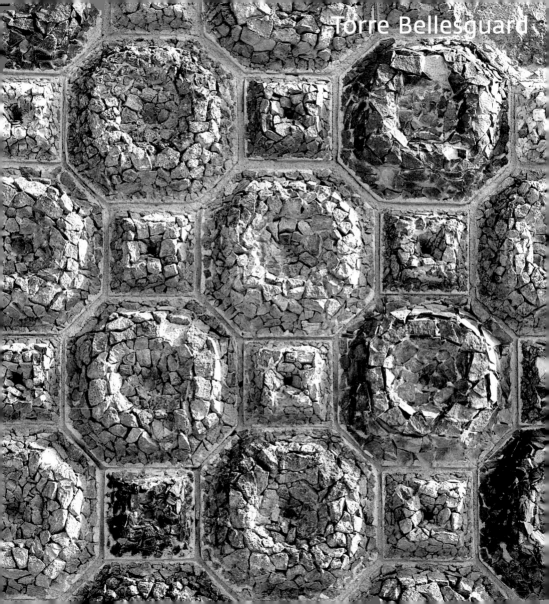

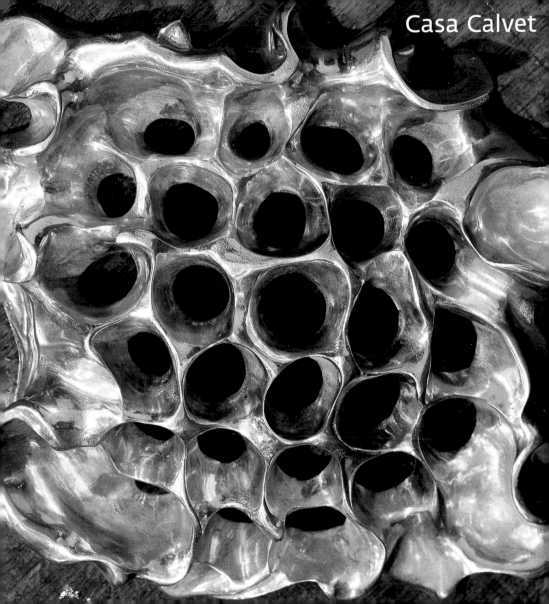

Casa Calvet

Casa Batlló

Palacio Episcopal de Astorga

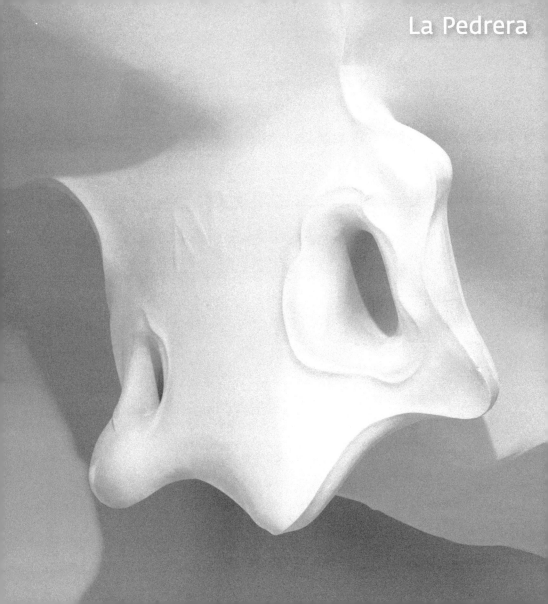
La Pedrera

Celler Güell

El Capricho

Basílica de la Sagrada Família

Casa Botines

Casa Vicens

GAUDÍ

Juan-Eduardo Cirlot

Introduction to Gaudí's architecture

There is a shroud of mystery surrounding Gaudí. In all probability, the first mist preventing us from gaining access to his work is the intrinsic mysteriousness of all genius and, at the end of the day, of all human spirit. The situation is complicated by the well-known fact that Gaudí wished to create an aura of silence around his persona, while, at the same time as maintaining this secretiveness —in other words, the annihilation of his fundamental values— gave expression and symbolisation to his moods and incredible mental power. Gaudí, despite his closeness to us in terms of time, rises before us surrounded by the revered magic which Jung called the *manna* personality. He is the wise man, the enlightened doctor —a trait that draws him close to Ramon Llull, another mysterious Catalan lost in the mists of time since the 13th century—; he is the artist whose superiority not only stems from both intellectual and spiritual possibilities but which sprouts, as a way of describing it, from the total and whole transformation of what he did and who he was. However, the second shroud of mystery lies in his particular era. Indeed, although close in time, his work was more a culmination of the long process that began with the rise of Christianity and pre-Romanesque art than the beginnings of our own times. And this, despite the fact that Gaudí's work, as an authentic creation of genius, or in other words, that which *generates*, gave us the rules and premonitions for a new concept in art, morphology and *pathos*. One thing, however, are these shapes rising from the heart of his work and another very distinct factor is the whole of this work as an expression of a period. The serious caesura that separates the Modernist period from ours could be explained by stylistic, social or political traits. Modernist art can be discovered in the shaping of the 19th century and appears indistinct in the work of some painters, especially that of Cézanne (1839–1906). We will say only one thing. The Modernist period still belonged, to a great extent, to the cultural eclecticism of the second half of the 19th century, based on admitting multiplicity and complexity, in short, that which is aged. In contrast, our era comes from a youthful demand, of a break with the past, of the reconquest of a new simplicity, of the rejection of the complex, to a greater or lesser extent. The mere contemplation of Gaudí's works, despite the profound inner and obvious links that join them, despite their unique expression of a particular era, tests this multiplicity and complexity that our feelings about the world want to reject. We say want because in this word there coexists, despite everything, a certain juxtaposition of distinct but nevertheless contradictory elements: functionalism and organic architecture and abstract painting and informal use of matter, non-figurative ascesis and surreal Baroque. The perceptible differences in Gaudí's creative work are undoubtedly due to perfectly justified distinct factors: the siting of the work and the objective respect the architect has for local peculiarities and technical traditions. It has been clearly observed that outside Catalonia he never used this a la Catalan brick vaulting, which are a precedent for current shells of buildings. Gaudí's work is also influenced by different eras: the Mudejar style of the earlier period and expressive morphology in the golden age of the Casa Milà, the Park Güell and the crypt of the church of the Colònia Güell. Nevertheless, at the same time, there is an intrinsic and I would dare to say "sacred monstrosity" in the variety of Gaudí's work that we would never find in Gropius or Moore, nor in the architects and artists who are recognised as having the most ability in variation and even contradiction, such as Frank Lloyd Wright or Picasso. This is because Gaudí's diversity does not lie in merely intellectual or instinctive terrain. The central point of the mystery of Gaudí's personality resides precisely in this innate ability to discover, reveal and recreate *an entire universe*. More than for reasons of his destiny or the influences of his upbringing, which must have brought him close to God enough to turn him into a mystical and pious person, it must have been the living discovery —compensated by his deep humility— of the divine factor that resided in his inner self. His own magnificent ability for invention that filled him with pleasure must have pushed him towards that Divinity with which he felt connected to the innermost depths of his whole being.

Caricature of Gaudí published in "La Publicitat" of the 13 June 1926

Soffit in the Parc de La Ciutadella produced when he was an assistant to Josep Fontseré →

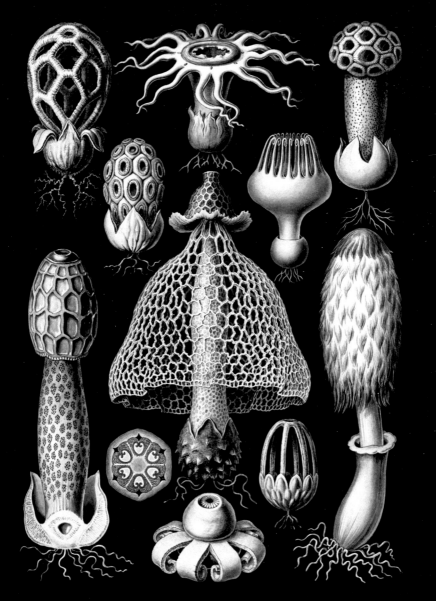

Ideological elements of his time

We have certainly not combed Gaudí's reading —who would be able to?— or even his travels. Nevertheless, on the other hand, we are sure that the explanation we seek could not be found in such sources. It has been seen that brilliant people, as yet another factor of their authority, have an incredible informative speed. This ability enabled Balzac, for example, to describe thousands of places and situations he saw without realising it with a "capacity of register" inaccessible to the majority of human beings. The ideological elements that "existed" in Gaudí's time must have been captured, deepened and analysed unconsciously and subliminally, continuously and profoundly effectively. Some of these elements have been described. For example, from his known studies, that of the theoretical works of Viollet-le-Duc (1814–1879), or the contact he kept with his favourite teachers: Francesc Llorens i Barba (1820–1872), who taught him philosophy and literature; and Pablo Milà i Fontanals (1810–1883), with whom he studied the theory and history of art. The latter's concepts and ideas are well known, based on integrating art into culture, thus breaking the isolation of artistic acts in order to incorporate them into daily life, a tendency which Gaudí had no option but be interested in. Regarding Llorens i Barba, we know that he preached a spiritualist doctrine, in which philosophy was not a specialisation but a piece of "complete knowledge". Some of this thinker's ideas are nearly enough to explain part of Gaudí's ideology: an ideology unformulated in written terms but patent and active in his architectural-expressive creativity. It is hard to believe, but for Llorens i Barba, "philosophical belief" was a *dark and subjective state*, a mystical doctrine if there is one. He believed, alternatively, in the "activity of substances subject to the first cause". And with this he approached, but without accepting everything that it involved, the monism of Ernst Haeckel, whose ideas and investigations "floated" around the air in Gaudí's formative years. Haeckel (1834–1919) fought for a biological conception of the universe in which matter was integrated, not in life, but in thought, a theory that Teilhard de Chardin, later on, often endorsed in part. On the other hand, Haeckel published many studies about natural forms (protozoans, radiolarians, medusas, etc.). When Folguera tells us that Gaudí, as well as history, studied "nature", we should suppose that he would have been interested in the most representative works of his time, in which the morphological obsession of pre-modernism had an abundant and nutritious grazing land. Between 1860 and 1890, Haeckel published numerous books of the morphology of natural beings, some of which were translated into Spanish, such as the *General Morphology of Organisms* (Barcelona, 1887). In our opinion, Gaudí's work shows an advance from traditional architecture towards new architectural structures based on mechanics and experiments such as the catenaries but, at the same time, and through the medieval and oriental tendencies in style, *openly enters the world of natural morphology which does not copy but transforms and integrates it into an architectural or structural-ornamental factor*. The colour used in his poly-

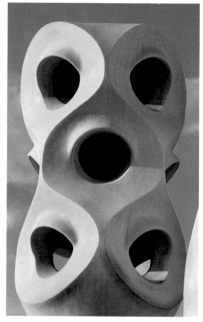

Detail of one of the tops of the flat roof of La Pedrera

chrome often reminds one more of the underwater flora and fauna than of the natural elements that could normally be seen. The rounding off of the bell towers of the Sagrada Família possess the qualities and drive of the medusa before that of the flower, and structures of radiolarian were clearly used by Gaudí on specific details, such as the peepholes of the Casa Calvet. There is no doubt, and this backs up what we have said of Gaudí's intrinsic complexity, that other very distinct ideological currents converge in his thought. This explains the spiritualist tendency, which had its roots in Celtic culture, the English Pre-Raphaelite doctrine (the Pre-Raphaelite Brotherhood was founded in 1848) and which, through the "Art and Crafts" movement of William Morris in 1861, rekindled by Ashbee in 1888, and the architects and decorators of the Glasgow School, reached Catalonia continuously to have a long-lasting influence. However, what could have been a dramatic ideological factor in Gaudí's time could be approached in other terms. If we were to refer to literature, we would see that through the naturalism of Zola (1840–1902) or by penetrating the cosmic symbolism of Melville (1819–1891) and the "willingness of power" of Nietzsche (1844–1900) it could be, in some way or another, transformed and "saved" by a mystic tendency. A Nietzsche redeemed by Parsifal, with the gaze fixed on the "Wild Mountain" or on the Montsalvat (or on Montserrat), could be very close to, as regards the general tone of the personality, the example of a Gaudí work. It must be emphasised in saying this, however, that we do not wish to do anything more than draw co-ordinates around the deeply unyielding figure of the great Catalan architect. A factor that should also not be underestimated in considering the ideological "façades" of a Gaudí piece is the repressed and intrinsically contradictory

Gaudí before La Pedrera in a drawing that imitated the poster announcing the opera by Wagner *Twilight of the Gods*

personality of the author of the Sagrada Família. The complexity of his work, which to a large extent resides in his time (still placed in nineteenth-century eclecticism, as we say), is also rooted in such contradictions or, in other words, divergent impulses. Sometimes they are miraculously combined —and then the works of the artist arise in a purer and more unitary form— but sometimes they juxtapose each other and we are witness to this kind of struggle on the seabed that certain Gaudí creations often evoke. Traditionalism and modernism, love for everything "Mediterranean" and brusque immersions to hinterlands that might be either Germanic or African (this African influence is strange by three men from Reus: Prim (1814–1870), winner of the Battle of Castillejos in 1860; Fortuny (1838–1874), painter of Moroccan themes and of Prim's heroic feat; and Gaudí, creator, with the project of the building for the Catholic Missions of Tangier. This construction had an unmistakable relationship —strangely and inexplicably— with the Hamite constructions of Togo and Kreis Següela). Added to that was refinement, almost worshipful of childish myths and a dream-like atmosphere, such as the pavilions in Park Güell. Also present was a tense surliness that was tremendously virile and dramatic, such as the tawny porticoes of leaning columns in the abovementioned park. We also find the calculating tendency, of "seeing the pressure lines" contrasted with pure imagination and his functional intuitions upsetting the expressionism. Nevertheless, the joining of opposites often resolves antinomies and this tendency towards mechanical expression seems to us to be more than an expression of a cold "technical" side to Gaudí, rather his faith in *everything* that was beautiful and divinely demonstrated. Furthermore, if in the contradictions of the great architect, there was a tendency that he could dominate, it was that of spiritualism. We have irrefutable evidence of this in Gaudí's own evolution, increasingly immersed in the calling that was plainly evident in his Sagrada Família work. Needless to say, therefore, in summing up, that the aesthetic ideology of Gaudí coincides with Schoenberg's thesis "to put into practice a scientific principle up to the final consequences". This is emphasised if we add that the "scientific principle" appears as a profane side of a revelation that was originally superior and extraordinarily mundane in its nature. Even in the radiolarians Gaudí saw God, as he did in the strength lines and the funicular polygons. The fact that he preferred the helicoid and parabola to the circle, triangle and square and to Plato's sphere is the fact that shows precisely the "difference" between classical culture and modernist *pathos* and the tearing apart of a tradition, resulting in mutation and the origin of a new world for mankind.

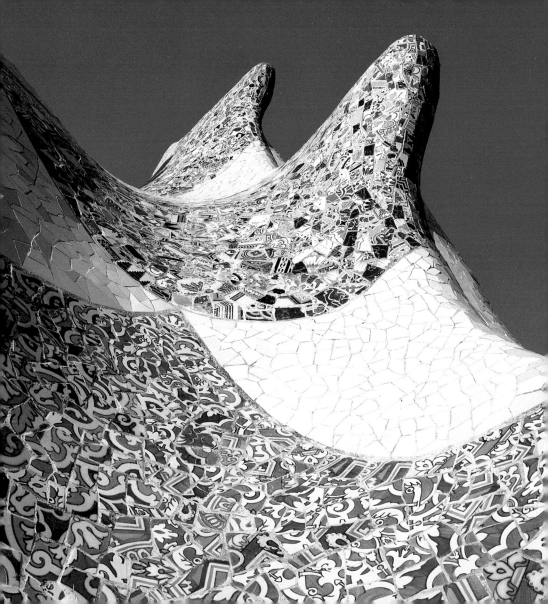

The early works (1878–1892)

Gaudí's early period is distinguished by the Mudejar influence, for alternating between this orientalist suggestion and medievalist emphasis, and for the progressive and growing appearance of the elements that correspond to Gaudí's mature period. Despite that, nevertheless it can be seen in his works that Gaudí put into practice two of his concepts that it is important to describe. When he was 26, Gaudí wrote in a diary, "The ornamentation has been, is and will be coloured. Nature does not produce anything that is monochrome or uniform in colour: neither vegetation nor in geology, nor in topography nor in the animal kingdom. The contrast in colour is always more or less alive and from this we are obliged to colour in part or all of an architectural piece, colouring that will perhaps disappear when the hand of time gives it another colour that is more befitting and precise for something old". Besides the total demonstration in favour of colour in architecture, what is really interesting in this statement is that Gaudí conceived architecture *within* nature, loyal to all its laws, even the external ones, that architecture always violated nature with its structures, it seems. The statement relating to colouring due to the "hand of time" is also important in that it corroborates, as if it were necessary to do so, the architect's sensitivity to colour-texture, to the qualities of the material. Another valuable feature of Gaudí is one described by Rubió who transcribed Gaudí saying that his greatest quality consisted in "knowing exactly whether something had to be higher or lower, flatter or more curved. This is nothing more than a quality for clairvoyance and I, luckily, can see it". He added, "I cannot do anything

Display cabinet by Gaudí for the Comella glove maker, exhibited at the Universal Exhibition of Paris of 1878

← Lamppost in Plaça Reial in Barcelona designed by Gaudí

about it. I just thank God and that is it". One can see an intuitive Gaudí here, who would use the mechanics to broaden his domain, but who "knew" the shape, as did the great sculptors-architects of the past. What Gaudí did not know was the *intensity* of this gift of knowing if "something had to be higher or lower, flatter or more curved", an intensity that helped him discover that the "interesting" shapes are not flat ones but concave or convex ones. This discovery was, nevertheless, made gradually and the works covering his early period are dominated by flat surfaces and traditional formulas enriched by decorative additions or also by the typical Gaudí structures such as the parabolic arches in the Casa Vicens (1883–1888). Here the glazed ceramic tile and wrought iron contribute to creating a vision of beauty. As regards the general structure of the building, Gaudí managed to enliven it by using all the resources found in the brick, a rich ground plan in angles and surfaces covered with strips of glazed ceramic tiles in relief. The grille with very naturalistic iron palms possesses a particular strength, so characteristic of Gaudí's work.

The project for the "Obrera Mataronense", of which only the stonework was ever completed, shows the casing of the stairway, in brick, on the exterior of the building and attached to it. This solution, in another stylistic sphere, would be taken up by Gropius in 1914 for his Werkbund factory in Cologne. Between 1883–1885, Gaudí built the "El Capricho" estate in Comillas (Santander), a work that maintained the tendencies shown in the Casa Vicens, but this time with more dramatic strength. The ornamentation on the tower that rises over the entrance portico is of a character that is simultaneously both "technical" and regressive and the geometry of the dome covering it possesses a quite violent intensity. It is an authentic work of cubism produced a full quarter of a century in advance and which clearly has the stamp of Gaudí's personality as a great master which does not bow to the more decadent and timid dictates of what we could call "orthodox modernism". In 1883, Gaudí, on accepting the appointment of architect of the Sagrada Família (Joan Martorell, architectural author of the Francisco de Paula del Villar project having turned the appointment down), acquired a responsibility that would end up identified with his destiny and absorbing all his creative energies when, from the outbreak of the first world war in 1914, he abandoned all profane work. Between 1884–1888, Gaudí worked intensively for Eusebi Güell, the illustrious figure he had first met in 1878 and who was to be his main client and patron. For Güell he built the palatial house in Nou de la Rambla Street, where he used funicular arches at the entrances and where he structured spaces of great monumental dimensions and strange articulations that are very close to, or even anticipate, some of those by Behrens. In this work Gaudí appears as the inventor of decorative or architectural elements conceived as sculptures, both in the wrought iron grilles of the entrance and in the geometrical chimneys that provide a pronounced magical air to the building's flat roof. Already appearing in these chimneys is the characteristic covering of pieces of glazed ceramic tile creating abstract compositions. Gaudí also designed the furnishing as he had done in the Casa Vicens. He also built the Pedralbes pavilions for Güell, highlighted by the value of the wrought ironwork with the "Dragon", which could, in all honesty, be considered as the direct ancestor of all the iron sculpture that was produced so much during the twentieth century, starting from the works of Gargallo and González.

Portrait of Eusebi Güell i Bacigalupi (1846–1918)

This early period also corresponds to several important buildings in which the artistic and personal influence of Gaudí is still not shown with the invasive strength of the following period. Between 1888–1890 he built the Theresan College in Ganduxer Street, Barcelona, with

monumental faces of brick rhymed by parabolic arches and in which still persists a certain Mudejar style. Between 1889–1893 work began on the grand Episcopal Palace of Astorga (León) with its splayed portals, an austere construction in granite and which includes ceramic decoration on the second floor. 1891-1892 represents the building of the "Los Botines" in León, a work containing a naturalistic sculpture over the facade of St. George slaying the dragon. This is the first time we see Gaudí use, paradoxically, what he believed to be sculpture, in contrast to the great abstract sculpture represented by his architectural work in details and as a whole and without forgetting his own architectural values and technical advances. Parallel to these works, Gaudí worked on the Sagrada Família, firstly on the crypt (1884–1887), begun by Villar, and later on the apse, which maintains the neo-gothic style to a great extent and which rises to a height of fifty metres.

Watercolour (1878) of the project for the "Sociedad Cooperativa Obrera Mataronense" (left) and the bleaching warehouse of the same organisation

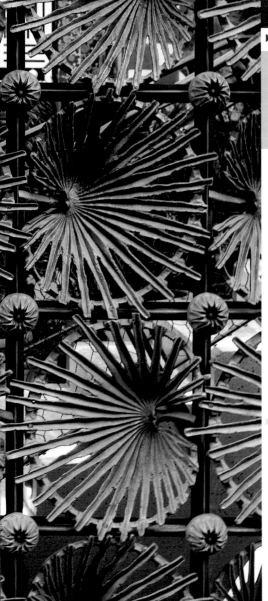

▶ **Barcelona**

Heritage Site of National Interest
UNESCO World Heritage Site

Casa Vicens

The Casa Vicens was the first important work undertaken by Gaudí. Situated in Carrer Carolines, it was built between 1883 and 1888 at the behest of the ceramic tile manufacturer Manuel Vicens Montaner. The Mudejar style —much used by Barcelona architects of the time— is recreated and surpassed in this building in which the combination of the tiles and bricks is expressed with an extraordinary strength.

▷ **Palm leaves**
The main motif of the iron gate –made in wrought iron by Joan Oñós from a clay model by Llorenç Matamala– are the palm leaves.

▶ **Casa Vicens** Carolines, 18. Barcelona

Isolated residential building built as a summer residence. It is structured on four levels: basement, ground floor and two upper floors, used as a storage area, living quarters, bedrooms and servant quarters, respectively.

The house has everything it needs for summer comfort, such as excellent ventilation on the inside and a large garden which originally included an artificial waterfall and the popular Santa Rita fountain, both demolished when the garden was dug up to make room for new constructions.

Considered as being Gaudí's first important piece of work, it is designed with great constructive simplicity, with a dominance of the straight line over the curve and with a notable emphasis of Arab-inspired aspects, such as the interior almocárabes, an interlaced design in plaster, and the outside solid brickwork.

The building is constructed of solid masonry walls, the floors with bricked up vaulting in their lowest part and with wooden beams on the higher floors and roofing.

Among the decorative work features the colourist ceramic covering on the facades, which reproduce the flora of the site alternating between white and green tiles, as well as the decoration of the gallery that opens out to the garden, the smoking room and the dining room, for which Gaudí designed part of the furnishings.

Registered in the Catalogue of Historic and Artistic Architectural Heritage of Barcelona. National Heritage Site since 1969.

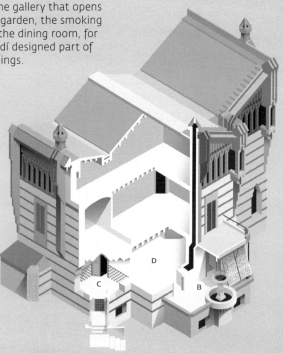

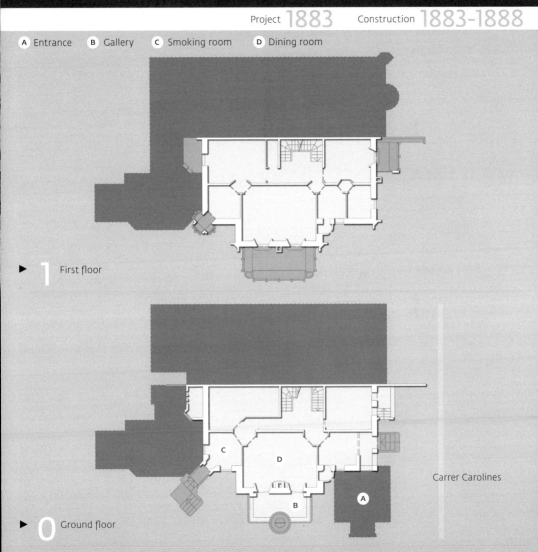

A Entrance   B Gallery   C Smoking room   D Dining room

▶ 1 First floor

▶ 0 Ground floor

Carrer Carolines

Casa Vicens

Moving bird
Over the chimney of the dining room, Gaudí placed a bird hanging from the ceiling that moved with the current of warm air.

Orient
Next to the polychrome moucharabies (page 47) orientalism is present in details such as the choice of cherries, of great symbolic meaning in the Orient.

Nature
The decoration with natural motifs, whether of plant life or animals, is the constant of this building, both outdoors and indoors where there are branches of cherry tree in polychrome plaster on the coffered ceiling of the dining room, stucco ivies on its walls, storks, flamingos and other birds on the lintels of the doors (page 45) or all combined as in the sleight of hand of the first floor (page 46).

French marigold
Gaudí found this plant species (*Tagetes patula*) on the site and turned it into the motif of the tiling on the façade and of the *fumoir*, the smoking room.

← EVEN THOUGH TODAY FLAT SURFACES DOMINATE, GAUDÍ WAS ABLE TO LIVEN UP THE FAÇADE THROUGH ALL THE RESOURCES OF BRICK AND SOME SURFACES COVERED BY STRIPS OF PROTRUDING CERAMIC TILES.

→ THE GALLERY IN THE DINING ROOM HAS RECENTLY BEEN RESTORED. HIGHLIGHTS INCLUDE THE FOUNTAIN AND THE LATTICEWORK SCREEN BETWEEN THE GALLERY AND THE GARDEN.

→
GAUDÍ PAYS SPECIAL
ATTENTION TO THE ANGLES
OF THE BUILDING IN ORDER
TO AVOID STIFFNESS. IN THE
PHOTOGRAPH, A DETAIL OF
THE BALCONY.
→
GAUDÍ CONCEIVED A TOTAL
DESIGN OF THE BUILDING
WHICH, AS WELL AS THE
METICULOUS CARE TAKEN
IN EACH EXTERIOR DETAIL,
INCLUDED THE INTERIOR
DESIGN WHICH IS HIGHLIGHTED
BY THE MURAL PAINTINGS AND
CABINETWORK.

P. 46-47
→
ON THE CEILING OF THE FIRST
FLOOR, TORRES MASSANA
PAINTED A "TROMPE L'OEIL",
CREATING THE ILLUSION OF
A CONNECTION WITH THE
EXTERIOR.
→
THE SMALL SMOKING ROOM
SHOWS THE ORIENTAL TASTE
OF THE PERIOD.

▶ **Comillas, Cantabria**

El Capricho

Situated in the Santander village of Comillas and built between 1883 and 1885 for Máximo Díaz de Quijano, the holiday villa El Capricho (The whim), was overseen entirely by the architect Cristóbal Cascante Colom, who followed the instructions sent by Gaudí from Barcelona. The work, in which the tendencies of the Casa Vicens are maintained, but with more dramatic force, is the confirmation of Gaudí's personal modernism.

▶ **Sunflower**
The sunflower of the tiling on the façade could be the symbol of the distribution of the interior spaces, whose daily activities would follow the path of the sun.

▶ **El Capricho** Land on the Palacio de Sobrellano, Comillas

Ⓐ Entrance Ⓑ Balcony Ⓒ Tower

A detached summerhouse built on a long, narrow, sloping site.

Gaudí encountered the difficult task of starting the project from Barcelona and without having set foot on the site. Despite this setback, he decided on a long building, taking advantage of the gradient to include three spaces: a lower ground floor used as a garage and store-room, a ground floor for the owner's home and an attic for the servants.

After the four single columns of the house which make up the entrance porch, he placed the front door, situated on the high-est side of the building and over which he built a slender watch tower overlooking the sea.

To break with the long and monotonous site, Gaudí designed the main facade with several projections, thus empha-sising its rhythm. He built the lower part of the building with stone and the rest with open brickwork, which he covered on the outside with glazed ceramic leaves and flowers of different colours.

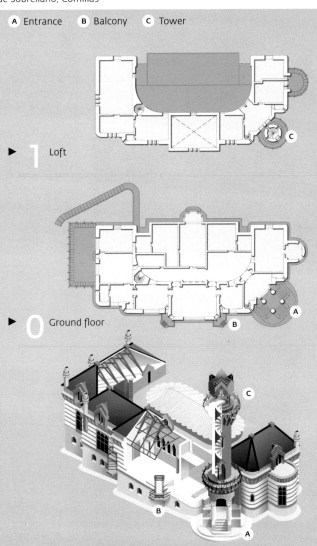

▶ **1** Loft

▶ **0** Ground floor

Stained glass

Gaudí reflected the owner's passion for music in diverse elements, both in the interior and exterior decoration. This is the case of the stained glass of the dragonfly with a guitar and that of the sparrow over an organ (page 55).

Musical window

It is also the case of the bench-balcony, where the counterweights of the sash window were metallic tubes that on rising or dropping were tapped by a rod and gave off pleasant musical sounds. Even the name of the building, El Capricho (the whim), evokes free and fantasy-filled musical composition.

→
AS WELL AS THE HORIZONTAL STRIPS OF THE BODY OF THE BUILDING, THE SUNFLOWERS COMBINED WITH LEAVES, GAUDÍ TOTALLY COVERS THE BRICK OF THE TOWER EMPHASISING ITS VERTICALITY.

→
THE EXTERIOR OF THE BUILDING IS CHARACTERISED BY THE USE OF BRICK ADORNED WITH THREADS OF GLAZED CERAMICS AND THE SUPERPOSITION OF THE CURVED SURFACE OVER THE STRAIGHT. ON THE OTHER HAND, THE TOWER –SIMILAR TO A MINARET– IS THE ELEMENT THAT MOST DEFINES THIS WORK, AND IS THE FIRST PRECEDENT OF AN ARCHITECTURAL SOLUTION THAT WOULD APPEAR IN FUTURE CONSTRUCTIONS SUCH AS BELLESGUARD OR THE PAVILIONS OF PARK GÜELL.

←
ON THE CAPITALS OF THE
SOLID COLUMNS OF THE
ENTRANCE PORCH APPEAR
PALM LEAVES AND SWALLOWS
CARVED IN STONE. TO DO THIS
THEY USED PLASTER MODELS
MADE BY GAUDÍ IN THE
BARCELONA WORKSHOP OF
LLORENÇ MATAMALA,
SCULPTOR AND
COLLABORATOR OF THE
ARCHITECT.
→
IN THE MUSIC ROOM, THE
STAINED-GLASS WINDOWS
SHOW ANIMALS PLAYING
INSTRUMENTS. IN THIS CASE,
A BIRD ON THE KEYS OF AN
ORGAN.

▶ **Barcelona**

Heritage Site of National Interest

Pavilions of the Güell Estate

From 1884 until 1887 Gaudí built the pavilions of the porter's lodge and the stables for the estate that the Güell family owned in Pedralbes. This work represents the first collaboration of the architect with Eusebi Güell, the Catalan businessman whose patronage would boost the architect's fame in a decisive way. These two pavilions feature, in particular, the dragon gateway, a sculpture of wrought iron designed by Gaudí himself. Originally, this dragon was polychromed and came alive by means of an ingenious mechanism.

▶ **Milestone**
In the garden, Gaudí placed this piece of stone with the initial of the surname of his patron, Eusebi Güell, and the year in which he began the construction of the pavilions: 1884.

▶ ## Pavilions of the Güell Estate Avda. de Pedralbes 7, Barcelona

A set of two auxiliary constructions, one designed as stables and exercise ring for horses, and the other as a lodge and dwelling for the caretaker. The first was built with just a ground floor plan and with access to the flat roof, whereas the second building has a ground and first floor, integrating both the workspace and the accommodation into a single building.

The structure of the two buildings is based on load-bearing walls, vaulting and parabolic arches. Gaudí used brick as the basic construction material and in some parts applied, for the first time, the ceramic *trencadís* mosaic, the practical system for outdoor covering made from broken tiles that are adapted to curved surfaces. Both pavilions bring to mind the aesthetic style present in his other contemporary buildings, as well as the predominance of the straight line over the curve.

Outside, the marked volume of the horizontal is crowned by several lanterns which, from the roofs, light up the interior vaulting through which the light is reflected.

In between the two buildings a spectacular wrought-iron gate stands out, cast in 1885 in the Barcelona workshop of Vallet y Piqué, and which represents a dragon, the immortal watchman of the property.

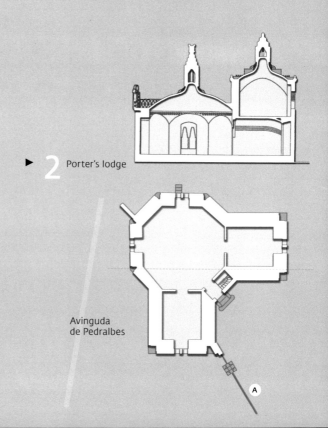

▶ **2** Porter's lodge

Avinguda
de Pedralbes

A

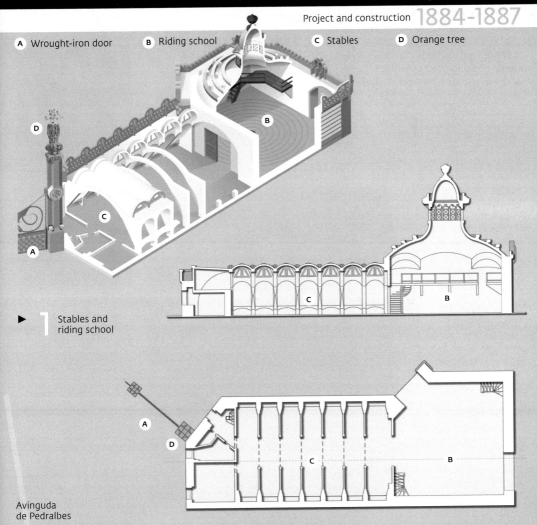

A Wrought-iron door   **B** Riding school   **C** Stables   **D** Orange tree

▶ **1** Stables and riding school

Avinguda de Pedralbes

▶ **Pavilions of the Güell Estate**

▷ Architecture and literature

As a background to the pavilions the mythical world of *L'Atlàntida* appears, the epic poem by Jacint Verdaguer that narrates how Hercules recovered the golden fruits from the Garden of the Hesperides guarded over by the dragon Ladon. Both elements are represented at the entrance by the antimony orange tree and the extraordinary wrought iron dragon. Other elements, such as the lyre of the grilles or the iron gate, abound in the relationship between literature and architecture. The golden englantine (*Rosa sempervirens*) was the prize awarded for the best patriotic poem in the *Jocs Florals*, the competition organised by the Barcelona City Council as a platform for the rebirth of Catalan culture in the 19th century.

▽ Fountain

In the original fountain, the sculpture was a representation of Hercules, who, along with the spout in the form of a dragon (page 68), refer to the episode in the Garden of the Hesperides.

▷ Dragon

The original dragon was polychrome, had glass incrustations in the eye and had a mechanism that gave it movement on opening the iron gate.

▲ The lyre

The lyre of the grilles is the symbol of poetry and, specifically, refers to the poet Jacint Verdaguer, winner of the *Jocs Florals* of 1877.

▷ Gilded fruits

The pillar of the entrance door is crowned by orange trees sculpted in stone that support another in antimony the fruits of which refer to the Garden of the Hesperides.

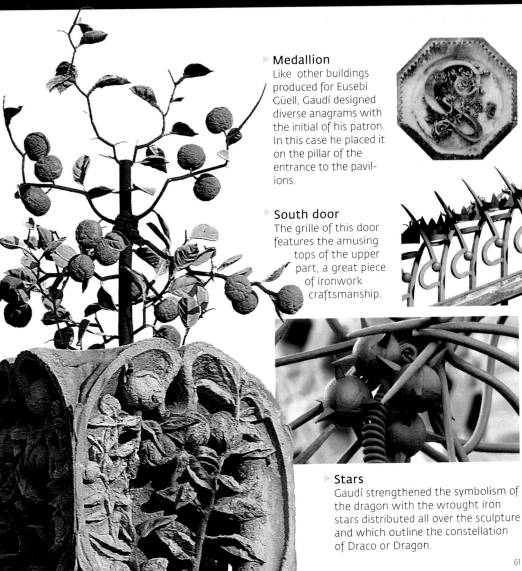

Medallion

Like other buildings produced for Eusebi Güell, Gaudí designed diverse anagrams with the initial of his patron. In this case he placed it on the pillar of the entrance to the pavilions.

South door

The grille of this door features the amusing tops of the upper part, a great piece of ironwork craftsmanship.

Stars

Gaudí strengthened the symbolism of the dragon with the wrought iron stars distributed all over the sculpture and which outline the constellation of Draco or Dragon.

P. 62-63
←
THE PAVILIONS ARE EVOCATIVE
OF MUDEJAR ARCHITECTURE
REINTERPRETED THROUGH
GAUDÍ'S MODERNISM.

→
THE GÜELL ESTATE REMINDS
ONE OF THE MYTHICAL
GARDEN OF HESPERIDES
WHERE HERCULES STOLE THE
GOLDEN FRUITS. THIS MYTH
WAS RECREATED IN
"L'ATLÀNTIDA" BY THE CATALAN
POET JACINT VERDAGUER, A
FREQUENT VISITOR TO THE
ESTATE. IN THE PICTURE, THE
ORANGE TREE MADE WITH
ANTIMONY.
→
PARABOLIC ARCHES FROM
THE OLD STABLES.

← →
THE ELEMENTS THAT
EMPHASISE THE VERTICALITY
OF A BUILDING IN WHICH
HORIZONTALITY DOMINATES
–AS OCCURS IN TRADITIONAL
ORIENTAL ARCHITECTURE– ARE
VERY IMPORTANT FOR GAUDÍ,
WHO MAKES A VISUAL
EXALTATION OF THE
FUNCTIONAL ELEMENTS OF THE
CROWNING, SUCH AS
CHIMNEYS, LANTERNS,
VENTILATION CONDUITS, ETC.

P. 68-69
→
NEXT TO THE PALACE OF
PEDRALBES IS THIS FOUNTAIN
WITH THE IRON SPOUT IN THE
FORM OF A CHINESE DRAGON.
AFTER BEING ABANDONED AND
HIDDEN, IT WAS FOUND AND
RESTORED IN 1983.
→
SECONDARY DOOR OF THE
ESTATE, ON THE OTHER SIDE OF
AVINGUDA DIAGONAL. IT WAS
RESTORED BY THE ARCHITECT
BUENAVENTURA BASSEGODA IN
1957.

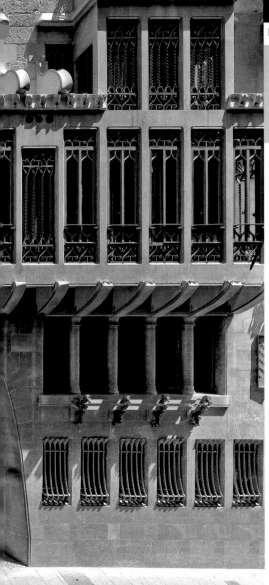

▶ Barcelona

Heritage Site of National Interest
UNESCO World Heritage Site

Palau Güell

In the Carrer Nou de la Rambla stands this majestic palace which Antoni Gaudí built between 1886 and 1888, for Eusebi Güell i Bacigalupi. Güell chose an unusual architect to erect not a house but a palace, which he would later show off to his acquaintances with concerts and exhibitions, etc. Gaudí's peculiarity expressed the new language of the bourgeoisie, created deliberately to tell a new history in which the patron had a key role. This palace, a rising metaphor, like Güell, extends from the dark basement of poverty to the festival of colour at the top culminating in the golden sunlight of wealth.

▶ Bows

Gaudí's graphic designs are always surprising. At the top of the façade appears the date 1888, the year of the completion of the palace and of the Universal Exhibition.

▶ **Palau Güell** Nou de la Rambla, 3-5. Barcelona

A family residence built in the historic centre of Barcelona and designed as an extension of another property owned by the Güell family in La Rambla and with which it was connected. It has six levels organised in different ways and for different purposes: the basement for stables, the ground floor for the reception, the mezzanine for the office, the first floor the home, the second floor the bedrooms and the third floor for the loft.

The basement features the helicoid ramp for the horses and the thick brick pillars which, together with the load-bearing walls, support the weight of the building. Of the rest of the building, mention must be made of its architectural conception, based on a very well lit central hall of over 80 m² and 17 m high, around which all the different rooms are positioned. The space is closed by a cupola, produced by a revolving paraboloid, which is covered with marble plaques full of holes allowing the light to filter through and resulting in an interesting luminous effect.

Gaudí used the parabolic arch, a geometric shape that appears constantly in all his later work, to a great extent and covered the ceilings of many rooms with wooden coffers, some worked with metallic elements with which they formed both decoration and structure. He also designed several functional elements, such as the flat roof chimneys, and took great care in working the materials well, such as the cast iron entrance doors that include the owner's initials on their upper section. Gaudí took full advantage of material that came from the owner's properties, such as the stone from Garraf with which the property's facades were built. The architect was also commissioned to design furniture, lights and stained glass windows, which he produced with the very best materials, ranging from delicate marbles to top quality woods, ceramics and multicoloured glass. With these materials he recreated atmospheres that were evocative of Gothic style and of Muslim art according to his own interpretation.

▶ First floor

Project 1886   Construction 1886–1888

A Entrance
B Main stairway
C Stables
D Office
E Lounge
F Chimneys
G Cupola

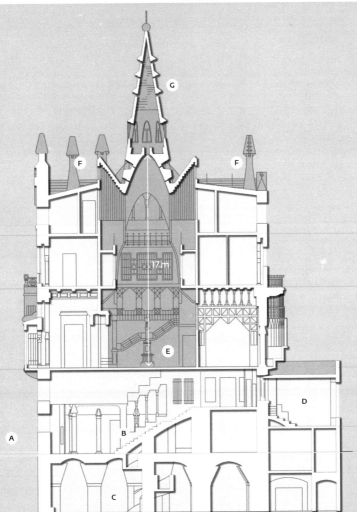

17 m

c/ Nou
de la Rambla

► Palau Güell

▷ Catalan coat of arms

Between the two entrance doors, in wrought iron, Gaudí places the Catalan coat of arms. In a bold design, the four bars (gules over gold) rise in a spiral over a cylinder and on both sides become winding ribbons. And the helmet, instead of the dragon or bat of the Catalan-Aragonese kings, is crowned by the Phoenix, symbol of rebirth, referring to the *Renaixença*, the Catalan cultural and political movement.

▷ Güell coat of arms

Gaudí designed a coat of arms for Güell based on the catenary form in which, from side to side of the crowning of the palace, one reads "Today lord, yesterday shepherd", a verse by Verdaguer, which refers to the plebeian origins of the count and abounds in the ideological programme of the renaissance of everything Catalan.

△ Weather vane

Over the slender lantern, Gaudí placed a weather vane in the shape of a bat, a heraldic symbol of the crown of Aragon, over a sun-compass and beneath the Greek cross.

▷ Initials

The "E" and the "G", initials of Eusebi Güell, appear on the palace doors, in another great design, in this case in wrought iron, by Gaudí.

→
GAUDÍ THOUGHT THAT
CROWNING BUILDINGS WITH A
RACHITIC ELEMENT WAS A TRUE
CARICATURE. ON THIS FLAT
ROOF HE PRODUCED HIS FIRST
"STAGE DESIGN" INTERVENTION,
A FORERUNNER OF CASA
BATLLÓ AND CASA MILÀ.

P. 78-79
→
IN ALL THE PALACE, GAUDÍ
USED FINE MATERIALS. IN
THE PICTURE, THE MARBLE
STAIRWAY IN THE MAIN
ENTRANCE.
→
THE CLOSURE OF THE GALLERY
OF THE REAR FAÇADE OF THE
PALACE DENOTES ANOTHER
VERY GENERALISED SOLUTION
IN COUNTRIES OF ORIENTAL
TRADITION. THE CLOSURE
ELEMENTS THAT PROVIDE
PRIVACY OF THE INTERIOR
SPACE ALLOW, HOWEVER, THE
FRESH AIR TO PASS THROUGH
AND VENTILATE ADEQUATELY.

→
DESPITE THE COMPLEX
ARCHITECTURAL STRUCTURE
OF THE GÜELL PALACE, THE
INTERIOR SPACES ARE
FLOWING.
→
THE CUPOLA IS MADE UP OF
PERFORATED HEXAGONAL
PIECES THAT ALLOW THE LIGHT
TO ENTER IN SUCH A WAY AS TO
IMITATE A CELESTIAL VAULT
THROUGH WHICH THE STARS
SHINE BRIGHTLY.

← INTERIOR OF THE GALLERY OF THE MAIN FLOOR. AS WELL AS THE PARABOLIC ARCHES ONE CAN SEE THE CARPENTRY WORK IN THE WINDOWS THAT ENABLES PRIVACY WITHOUT BEING CUT OFF FROM THE OUTSIDE.

← LIKE THE REST OF THE PALACE, THE WROUGHT IRON WORK IS EXQUISITE. THE ONE EMBRACING THE CAPITAL OF THE BEDROOM GIVES THE STONE LIGHTNESS AND MOVEMENT.

P. 84-85
→ THE BASEMENT STABLES WERE BUILT FROM THICK BRICK COLUMNS WITH FUNGIFORM CAPITALS.

→ TWO PARABOLIC ARCHES SUPPORTED BY A CENTRAL COLUMN CONNECT THE STABLES WITH AN INNER COURTYARD.

← THE CHIMNEY TOPS WERE RESTORED IN 1994 BY DIFFERENT PLASTIC ARTISTS.

→ ON THE ROOF A SERIES OF TWENTY SCULPTURAL CHIMNEYS SURROUND THE SKYLIGHT ON THE CENTRAL SALON.

▶ **Barcelona**

Heritage Site of National Interest

Theresan College

The building was constructed between 1888 and 1890 at the behest of Enric d'Ossó, the founding priest of the congregation of Theresan nuns. In contrast with other works, Gaudí was subject to strict economic controls. This condition explains the sober appearance of the college in which the architect uses a rational and severe language where the Mudejar style persists.

▷ **Handle**
Gaudí, admirer of the mystical poetry of the Spanish Golden Century and therefore that of Saint Theresa, designed handles in the form of a T, the saint's initial.

▶ **Theresan College**   Ganduxer, 85. Barcelona

A school building (convent, college and boarding school) begun in late-1888 by an unknown architect, it was shortly after entrusted to Gaudí, when the building was at the height of the second floor. Despite this factor imposing the ground plan on his work, rectangular and very long, he was able to complete the work in little less than a year after amending the original project substantially.

The Theresan College has four floors (ground floor plus three upper floors) designed as three longitudinal spaces, the central one being a skylight. With this system Gaudí achieved the entrance of light from the top floor through to the ground floor and which in its trajectory, lit up all the adjoining rooms.

He used the parabolic arch for both the outside and the inside. They stand out in the corridors that support the light well, forming spaces of remarkable architectural, aesthetic and luminescent resolution. The main materials he used were stone and solid brick, of a low cost but nevertheless very serious, contrasting with the elaborate wrought iron and ceramic work.

Gaudí was also commissioned to develop the surrounding area, designing a huge garden according to his own particular naturalist way of conceiving spaces, in which he planted palm trees and pines surrounding the paths and stone benches. The main part of the garden disappeared with the construction of the Barcelona Ring Road.

Although the Theresan College suffered a great deal of damage in 1936, when it was attacked and pillaged, it still continues functioning as an educational centre.

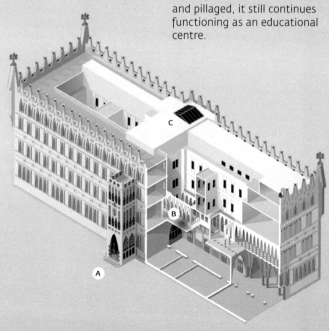

A Entrance   B Gallery   C Chandelier

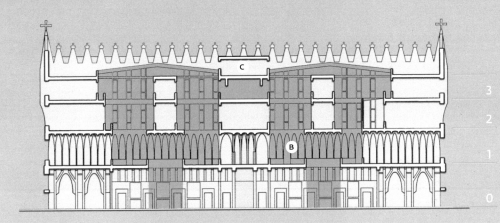

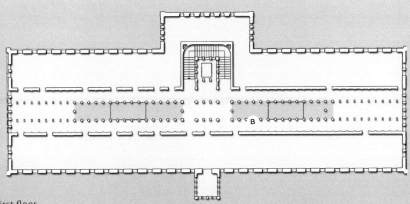

► 1 First floor

▶ Theresan College

▸ Theresan coat of arms

Beneath a doctoral cap, symbol of the saint, appears Mount Carmel (symbol or prayer) crowned by the cross (sacrifice). The star in the mountain (the teaching that comes from prayer) is also the symbol of the Virgin of Carmen. On the left of the mountain, the heart of Jesus, crowned with thorns, gives off flames of love; and on the right, a heart pierced by the arrow of divine love represents that of Theresa, who also returns the love received.

▸ Four-armed cross

The pinnacles are crowned by this cross-rose of the winds, which Gaudí would convert into a constant in his later works.

▸ Doctoral cap

The battlements are also crowned by the doctoral cap, symbol of the saint due to her being a Doctor of the Church.

▸ Entrance grille

Masterpiece of wrought iron work, it also reproduces all the symbols of the Theresan coat of arms. This grille only opens from the inside.

←
DOOR OF THE MAIN
ENTRANCE. IT IS MADE UP OF
THREE VERY THICK PANELS AND
IN THE CENTRAL PANEL THE
COMPANY COAT OF ARMS IS
REPRESENTED.
→
HELICOIDAL COLUMN OF THE
INTERIOR BUILT IN BRICK.

→
THE CORRIDOR OF CATENARY
ARCHES OF THE GROUND
FLOOR HAVE DOORS AT BOTH
ENDS THAT DRAW THE SAME
ARCH WITH A GREAT PIECE OF
CARPENTRY AND GLASS WORK.
→
THE EXTERIOR AUSTERITY OF
THE BUILDING CONTRASTS
WITH THE WARM INTERIOR
ATMOSPHERE ACHIEVED DUE
TO A MASTERLY DISTRIBUTION
OF NATURAL LIGHT, AS CAN BE
OBSERVED IN THE PASSAGEWAY
OF THE CLOISTER ON THE FIRST
FLOOR.

▶ Astorga, León

Heritage Site of National Interest
St James Way Heritage

Episcopal Palace
of Astorga

In 1887, Joan Baptista Grau, the bishop of
Astorga, entrusted Antoni Gaudí, his friend and
countryman, with the construction of the Episcopal palace. The architect, who worked on
this building from 1889 until 1893, abandoned
the work after the death of the bishop, its
main champion. Gaudí worked out the project
for the palace from books and photographs of
León-style architecture and he used local building materials, such as chalk and granite from
the Bierzo region. Nevertheless, the building
shows the inappropriate and suggestive Gothic
style of a fairytale castle.

▶ Episcopal signs
of authority
The zinc angels of the
garden are carriers of
some of the bishops'
signs of authority, such
as the mitre or crozier.

► **Episcopal Palace of Astorga** Plaza Eduardo de Castro. Astorga, León

A Entrance B Library C Lounge D Moat E Loft

Detached building constructed in a particular Gothic style and very much in harmony with the local architecture. It has four levels: the lower-ground floor (for the archive and storeroom), the ground floor (that includes the vestibule, reception, conference room, secretary's office, several offices and the notaries' and clerks' rooms), the first floor (for the chapel, the throne room, dining room, library, the bishop's private quarters and several bedrooms for guests) and the attic (for the servants).

The palace is built around load-bearing walls and columns, and features the abundant use of flat brick ogival and rib vaulting, the type of vaulting dominant throughout the building.

An outstanding feature of the exterior is the entrance portico, whose voussoirs, enlarged in the form of a fan, frame the three entrance doors. Also dominant are the sober stone walls, the many windows, the circular towers and the wide ditch surrounding the building, enabling light to enter the basement and through which the three service doors can be reached.

Museum of the Ways since 1963.

◄ Ground floor

▶ Entrance porch

The originality of this porch lies in the three large trumpet-shaped arches, not at all usual in Gaudí's buildings, and which present an enormous difficulty for the placing of the gigantic keystones. This part was added by the architect in the course of the work.

▶ Bishop's coat of arms

Over each of the large towers that flank the main door, Gaudí had the coat of arms of Bishop Grau sculpted, who had entrusted him with the palace.

▶ Angels

Although they are now in the garden, the three zinc angels manufactured in Asturias in 1913 should have crowned the building according to the 1887 project.

→

AS IN OTHER UNDERGROUND SECTIONS BY GAUDÍ, THIS LOWER GROUND FLOOR EXUDES SOBRIETY AND SOLIDITY. IN THIS CASE THE OGIVAL VAULTING HAS BRICK RIBS IN HERRINGBONE ARRANGEMENT.

→

IF ON THE EXTERIOR GAUDÍ USES AUTOCHTHONOUS MATERIALS SUCH AS SLATE OR GRANITE FROM BIERZO, IN THE RIBS OF THE VAULTING AND THE CORNICES OF THE NEO-GOTHIC HALLS HE USES PIECES OF CERAMIC FROM JIMÉNEZ DE JAMUZ, ALSO A TOWN IN LEÓN.

▶**León**

Heritage Site of National Interest
St James Way Heritage

Casa Botines

The Fernández-Andrés company, the successor to Homs & Botinás (the surname which when Hispanicized, comes out as "botines" with which the building is known), entrusted to Gaudí, through Eusebi Güell, the construction of a house in León. The building, on which work began in 1892, was erected in just ten months. In the lintel of the door, the Catalan architect placed a naturalist sculpture of St. George slaying the dragon.

▶ Saint George and the dragon

Sculpture by Llorenç Matamala over the main entrance. In 1953, on being restored, beneath the pedestal, a metal tube appeared with the original plans.

▶ Casa Botines Plaza de San Marcelo. León

A detached residential building with a storeroom and shop, with an almost rectangular ground plan and with a medieval look very similar to that of the neighbouring Episcopal Palace of Astorga.

Erected in the historic centre of León, with the Casa de Botines the architect strove to overcome the historical styles, with the aim of presenting a modern concept of architecture and combining the utilitarian, constructive and artistic aspects. There are seven levels with differing uses: the lower-ground floor is the storeroom, the ground floor the shop, the first floor the owners' home, the next two floors for rented accommodation, the attic as a storeroom and a space for the servants' quarters.

The building is structured with load-bearing walls on the floors, whereas in the basement there are iron pillars, only 18 cm thick with which Gaudí obtained a wall-free structure, ideal for commercial transactions.

The outside is notable for the grey granitic stone, which came from the area, arranged in irregular ashlar and discontinuous lines. The four corners are finished with circular towers with which the architect managed to provide the facades with the visual turn and enable light to enter. The roof is grey slate, a traditional insulator from the snow and rain, and includes six skylights for lighting up the inner courtyards.

The works management, in the absence of Gaudí, was headed by the Catalan constructor Claudi Alsina, who placed the only sculpture in the house over the front door. It is the work of Antoni Cantó and Llorenç Matamala, and was made in Barcelona and represents St. George fighting the dragon. The door is closed with an imposing iron grille, presided over by the image of a lion, the animal that brings to mind the name of the city.

The building was bought in 1931 by the Caja de Ahorros y Monte de Piedad de León, a savings bank, and was later owned by the Caja España, the bank that restored it between 1994 and 1996 and made it their company headquarters.

Heritage Site since 1969. Integral part of the St. James Way since 1999.

Plaza
San Marcelo

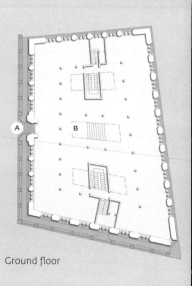

▶ 0 Ground floor

A Entrance   B Shop   C Loft

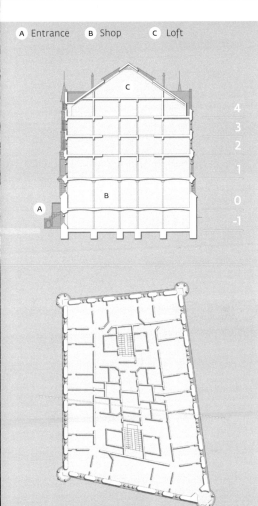

First floor

Initials
On the upper part of the entrance doorways to the homes one can read the initials of the founder of the business: Joan Homs.

Lion
Over the front door, the roaring lion, another excellent piece of wrought iron work, symbolises the city and kingdom of León.

Peephole
A common form in the designs of Gaudí, the spiral, acquires even more dynamism with the crosspieces of plant life forms that it gives off.

→
PASSAGE FROM LOFT TO THE
TOWER WHERE ONE CAN SEE
THE WOODEN FRAMEWORK
THAT SUPPORTS THE ROOF .
→
IRON PILLARS OF JUST 18 CM
THICKNESS, WITH WHICH
GAUDÍ ACHIEVED A STRUCTURE
FREE OF WALLS AND OPTIMUM
FOR COMMERCIAL
TRANSACTIONS.

The period of maturity (1892–1914)

All classifications by period are arbitrary and conventional: this has been repeated *ad nauseam* and if, on the one hand, it were never repeated again, on the other, one could still never escape from these classifications even though pointing out their relativity. Gaudí had a special gift reserved only for the great creative artists —something that can be seen from studying biographies and artistic careers in detail—, his inventive power increasing uninterruptedly almost until the end of his life. In 1892, when he was forty, he began to show signs of a particular originality ("returning to the origin" according to Gaudí himself) which can only be judged as abrupt and revolutionary. The building project for the Catholic Missions in Tangier, with its seven central cones, apart from being connected to the African works we mentioned before, constructs a "cosmic image" or, in other words, a symbolic "model" of universal totality. This aspiration, within Gaudí's morphological inventions and technical experimentation, stayed with him in his inner self, later to appear in his projects for the church of the Colònia Güell and in his triumphal image of the Expiatory Temple of the Sagrada Família. The cone, or the parabolic or spindly tower, is the essential expressive element of this conception, along with the ground plan distribution of the whole that symbolically defines the idea of totality (centre surrounded by a series of four or seven elements). But while Gaudí advances along the path of his inventive creativity his personality is transformed and if his religiousness is confirmed, his disinterest in the external increases and his biographers, or those that still remember him, can test the contrast between the young Gaudí who was

Watercolour of the project for the Franciscan Catholic Missions of Tangier produced in 1893, which, although never undertaken, shows similarities to the Temple of the Sagrada Família

almost a dandy and the mature Gaudí, indifferent to getting dressed or to his living conditions, his relationships with others and all that goes with it. Above all, from the death of his father in 1906, and in the last twenty years of his life, he threw himself into his work and thought so much that he forgot that he still had a body and lived in a material world inhabited by fellow beings, but similar only on the outside.

Gaudí's mysticism, however, never abandons the sensual, even glorious evaluation of natural morphology despite his abandonment of himself. Without sharing Haeckel's monism, mentioned before, we are nevertheless reminded of him and specifically, his conception of the world of which it has been said, "approximated organic and inorganic nature, science and religion, thought and the material world", almost finally identifying the physical and the psychic. Gaudí's intensity sometimes appears to produce a similar result, but in Gaudí's ideology there was, we know, a perfect submission to orthodoxy. In this way, the expressions are more unconscious, symbolic and even repressed (like Beethoven's cordiality). After the Casa Calvet (1898–1900), a work with lively personal accents within general containment, comes the insistence on the neo-gothic of Bellesguard, with vaulting a la Catalan and the inspired use of the grille (1900–1909). We must now refer to Gaudí's two main collaborators, whose contribution should in no way be ignored. Francesc Berenguer (1866–1914), as can be seen from his Garraf work, despite not having an architectural qualification, was able to help him mainly, perhaps, in the structural or mechanical side. On the other hand, Josep M. Jujol (1879–1949), "architectural painter", had an important role in the decoration of some exteriors and interiors, such as that of the Casa Batlló, in Passeig de Gràcia, Barcelona (1904–1907), the facade of which reminds one of Monet's *Water Lilies*, with their irregularly distributed discs, their deformed colourings of the flat surfaces (violets, lilacs, blues and greens), their marvellous chimneys, the sculptural forms, Moore-like by now, of the flat roof apron or the interior, etc. It is perhaps in this period when the modernist aspect of Gaudí's work really stands out the most, justifying the inclusion, though out of place, of the great master in the movement and of which Pevsner, knowing what we know, said in *Pioneers of Modern Design*, "Gaudí is the most significant artist of Art Nouveau… the only genius that this movement has really produced".

In the extremely important works described below, Gaudí's formal inventiveness is shown very clearly as is its transformation in expressive values of any structure. The flat surface, on being deformed, on warping, acquires values related to ovoid shapes and in this way anticipates the sculpture of Arp, Brancusi, Moore or Pevsner. The formal sections of these elements or the schemes that make up flat forms, such as the glass doors in the Casa Milà (1906–1912), provide the forms that would be abundant in the art of Arp, Miró or Calder. Gaudí conceives the architectural work as a living reality that he had to be able to "touch", as a manner of speaking, with his hands and really shape it. One is reminded of the craftsman-like sculpting ability of his elders which he transformed, magnified and integrated into his art, and there is room for a miraculous intuitiveness of what would reign in the art world over the next fifty years, produced at a time when the fauves were the most "advanced" (the orientalist decorative style of Matisse) and in which Picasso began his pink period. For reasons of repression, Gaudí plunged his sensuality into the springs of his spirit and from there it gushed, converted into visions such as that of the attic and roofing of the Casa Milà, which defied all logic and demonstrated his interest in geodesic lines. If this building, with its seven stone folds, which seem as much like the structure of Montserrat as they do of the insane rhythms of Van Gogh, is something quite unusual and prodigious, then the apex breaks all boundaries. Added to that, there are the architectural technical innovations, such as the elimination of interior walls and circular corridors that underline the biomorphic nature of the whole, revitalising the geology of the other side which is further enlivened by the prodigiously dynamic wrought iron grilles on the balconies. These pre-dated not just the archaic works in iron of the years between 1925–1930, but also the informal metallic forms of Claire Falkenstein, who recognised this in a "Homage to

Gaudí". Regarding the chimneys and hatchways of the roofing, the helicoid and undulating forms predominate, softened by the lyrical white nuances of the tiling. There are also perforated spaces such as those which years later would be present in the expressive work of Moore and Hepworth.

In 1898, Gaudí had begun his studies for the church of the Colònia Güell in Santa Coloma de Cervelló, studies which lasted for ten years. The crypt, which is the only constructed part, was built between 1908 and 1914, the year in which Gaudí decided his work on this building was finished due to external reasons. A hyperboloid roof, inclining columns whose direction follow that of the strength lines marked by the push of the land and the weight of the roof are the crypt's main features, along with the use of vaulting *a la Catalan* and the incorporation of star-shaped stained-glass windows and strangely beautiful ceramic elements. The building is possibly Gaudí's masterwork in terms of overcoming complexity and in its strangeness *per se*. In Gaudí the hyper-rational and the irrational combine, the calculator who attracted attention in his youth and the intuitive one who "saw" the "best form" of a perfectly independent *Gestalt Theory*. It is in this crypt where these two facets of Gaudí's thought are best integrated. On the one hand, the architectural subversion that manifests itself in the leaning columns and their somewhat disturbing ambiguous relationship with nature, and on the other hand, the architect achieves a clear serenity that both springs from the visibility of its mechanical conceptions and from the conscience of the rhythm with which the resulting forms are articulated by. This work is also profoundly traditional in the deepest sense of the word. It is opposed to both the arbitrary establishment of the new and rootless and to the pursuit of the old and routine or through a lack of creative imagination. The synthesis of ordered articulation or of live and animated detail and the formal totality of the whole is extraordinary and it is almost impossible to put into words. Only with an attentive and sensitive contemplation of this crypt, in which the principles and very best results of Gaudí's tectonics are concentrated, immersing oneself in its crystalline and organic atmosphere, and with its "power" of infinite unfolding, can we get near to the expression that Gaudí demonstrated in a unique way. Brick and coloured glass, geometry and "gestures" or impulses that materialise in the structures, ancestral religiousness and a "displaced" or "other" sense or the architectural image all combine and multiply amongst themselves. The synthesis of contradictions, the *coincidentia oppositorum* is now attained and, in consequence, the keen observer will find serenity mastering the tormented and order within the imaginative of this work, whose high church would perhaps have been, once again, the surpassing of the superior.

Simultaneously, between 1900 and 1914, above all between 1900 and 1903, Gaudí worked on the urbanisation of the Muntanya Pelada area, creating the Park Güell there, representing another outstanding aspect of his art. His expression here is undoubtedly freer and in the contradictory elements, instead of combining them, he uses contrast with great frequency. On the one hand, we have an almost child-like world of beauty with magical colours on the main steps and in the entrance halls with their prodigious roofing which are like the sublimation and sweetening of the scaled roof of the Casa Batlló. Firstly, there is the hypostyle hall with its Grecian style interpreted a little like Stravinsky interprets the pre-classical musicians and the embellished ceiling with collages made from fragments of glasses, bottles and dolls, which it has been said may be the work of Jujol. Then, in contrast, the violence of the stone porticoes with leaning columns, typical of Gaudí, with a rhythm of the snake of Evil, and the containing walls with tree-shaped columns which are continued in the abstract caryatids of the higher part of the park, with abrupt and pointed rocks. Later on we see the sinuous beauty of an undefined and infinite rhythm of the bench coated in broken glazed tiles, in abstract compositions, exactly coeval with Kandinsky's first abstract works. To sum up, the whole park, with its contradictory beauty and unique strength in the world, is an extraordinary spot where man's spirit truly breathes.

Güell Bodegas

The Güell Bodegas, in Garraf, a coastal town situated between Barcelona and Sitges, were built between 1895 and 1901. Francesc Berenguer, assistant to Gaudí, was, more than a collaborator, co-author of this building that, for some time, was even attributed to him completely. Eusebi Güell, owner of vineyards in the county of El Garraf, had these bodegas built to bottle the wine he exported to Cuba.

Garraf

In the concierge's office, the inscription "Garraf" not only refers to the name of the county, but also to the lyrical poem of the same name first performed in 1892 in the Palau Güell (music by García Robles and libretto by Picó i Campanar) and the author of which who remained on the sidelines was Güell himself, and was based on the grand project of the count to take water from the underground springs of Garraf to the then parched Barcelona.

121

▶ **Güell Bodegas** Carretera Barcelona-Sitges, km 25. Garraf, Sitges

The Güell Bodegas are made up of two buildings: the reception area and the aptly named cava, or cellar. It has a rectangular ground plan and the elevation reveals a pyramidal section that stands out for the way in which the walls are transformed into the roof. It has three levels: the ground floor, used as the depot and bodega; the first floor, for the owner's home and the second floor, for a chapel and viewpoint with views over the Garraf massif and the Mediterranean Sea. What stands out here is the abundant use of the parabolic arch and of those deliberately designed elements, such as a small and slender bell tower, chimneys with naturalist finishes and the inclusion of the letter G of the owner carved into the stone on the facade. The property is built from local stone, in harmony with the rocky landscape of the setting.

The reception area is a building of discrete proportions, made in stone and brick, giving an interesting view over the main door. This is closed off by an iron grille that includes a mesh of the same material, reminding one of the fishermen's nets.

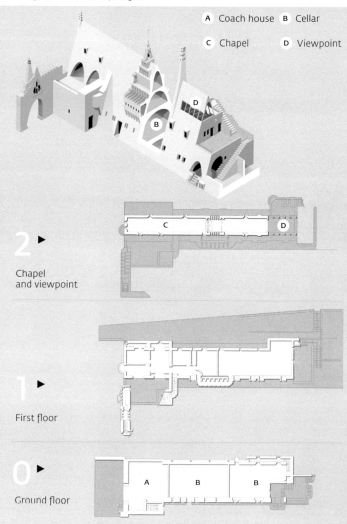

A Coach house **B** Cellar
C Chapel **D** Viewpoint

2 ▶
Chapel and viewpoint

1 ▶
First floor

0 ▶
Ground floor

Chapel

Portico-viewpoint
Supported by slender inclining pillars that enable one to lean out, this viewpoint of catenary arch and vault is also the portico of the chapel, and over its tympanum Gaudí placed the anagram of Count Güell in a new graphic design of great quality.

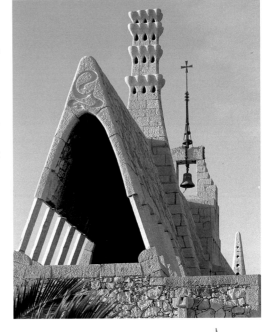

Wine glasses
Gaudí always gave importance to humble elements such as chimneys. In this case the piled up glasses refer to the product that was stored in the building.

Wrought iron vessel
Güell exported his wine in boats of the Compañía Trasatlántica, owned by his father-in-law the Marquis of Comillas. The shape of the iron entrance gate reminds one of the bow of a boat.

→
THE EXTERIOR OF THE
BUILDING IS CONSTRUCTED IN
MASONRY OF GREY STONE
FROM THE GARRAF. THE SAME
MATERIAL WAS USED BY GAUDÍ
IN OTHER BUILDINGS IN
BARCELONA.

→
EUSEBI GÜELL STORED
A WINE OF DUBIOUS QUALITY
IN THE GARRAF BODEGAS
WHICH HE EXPORTED TO
CUBA IN THE BOATS OF THE
TRANSATLANTIC COMPANY.

Casa Calvet

Pere Màrtir Calvet was the promoter of this property, which was built in Carrer Casp in Barcelona between 1898 and 1900. This time Gaudí recreated Catalan Baroque in this markedly nineteenth-century building. In 1900 the Casa Calvet won the prize which, for the first time, Barcelona City Council awarded to the best building. The threshold of the door is framed by the letter "C" and the cypress tree, a symbol of welcome, on its upper part, and on both sides by two sewing mill looms which refer to the industrial activity of Calvet.

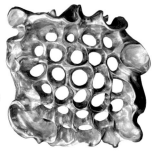

▶ **Peephole**
Gaudí achieved this organic form, which reminds one of a honeycomb, sinking his fingers repeatedly into a clay base.

▶ **Casa Calvet** Casp, 48. Barcelona

A building of commercial premises and homes built between dividing walls in one of the streets considered select at the time of the new Eixample district of Barcelona. It is structured from six levels (basement, ground floor, first, second, third and fourth floors) which are designed along the same lines of contemporary buildings of that time: the ground floor fused for the family business, the first floor for the owner's home and the other floors for rent.

Concerned with the correct interior lighting, Gaudí built a large stairwell that joined two wells, thus achieving the interior illumination of the floors. The interior features the decoration of the vestibule and the design of the lift, as well as the solving of distinct functional elements, such as the doorknobs, peepholes and handles. Also of note are the management office and the offices of the owner's textile company, for who Gaudí designed armchairs, tables and chairs adapted to the anatomy of the human body.

The basic construction materials were stone, ceramics, iron and wood, all top quality.

Casa Calvet is today a private home and the ground floor has housed, for some years now, a restaurant that has preserved many of the original features designed by the architect. It has been a Cultural Asset of National Interest since 1969.

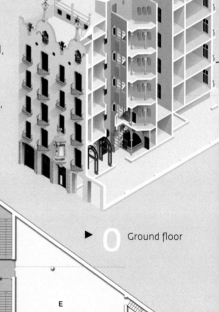

▶ 0 Ground floor

A Entrance   **B** Vestibule   **C** Lift   **D** Offices   **E** Courtyard   **F** Rear façade

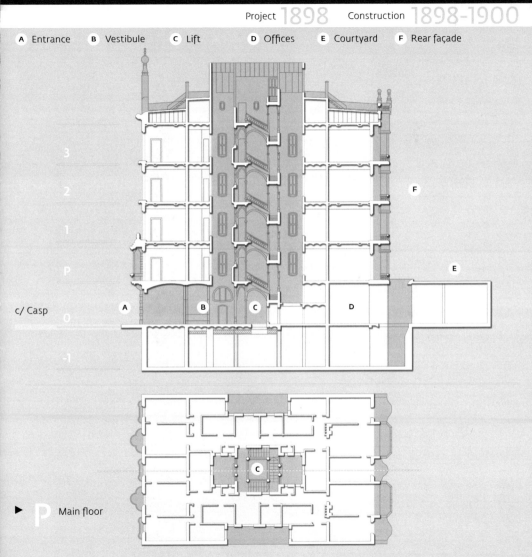

c/ Casp

▶ **P** Main floor

▶ **Casa Calvet**

▲ Textile reels

The columns of the entrance door are textile reels, the industrial activity that Calver worked in.

▶ Furniture

Casas and Bardés, Gaudí's regular carpenters, worked in oak wood with dovetailed pieces without nails or screws. As was the custom, Gaudí designed wooden furniture adapted to its function with a minimum of material.

▼ Mushrooms

The Gaudian designs of the balcony remind one of the form of the latticed stinkhorn (*Clathrus ruber*), and show the owners keenness for mycology.

▲ ▶ Offices

Many of the items of furniture for the offices and shop are conserved today in the restaurant that occupies the ground floor of the building.

▶ Baroque

As Gaudí stated, the building is inspired by Catalan Baroque. Over the gallery, with a great many details sculpted and in wrought iron with naturalist motifs, two horns of plenty and a dove that feeds its two chicks symbolise the fortune that Calvet left his family.

→

FOR THE FIRST TIME, GAUDÍ BUILDS A HOUSE FOR SEVERAL DWELLERS. THE FACADE CONTAINS MANY SCULPTURAL DETAILS AMONG WHICH FEATURE BUSTS OF THE PATRON SAINTS OF VILASSAR, THE BIRTHPLACE OF CALVET, AND THE TWO HORNS OF ABUNDANCE WHICH CROWN THE DAIS, A MYTHOLOGICAL OBJECT MUCH USED AT THE TIME AS A SYMBOL OF OPULENCED.

→

OVER THE ARCH OF THE VESTIBULE A CATALAN FLAG CARRIES INSCRIBED IN CATALAN THE GREETING "HAIL THE VIRGIN MARY FREE OF CONCEIVED SIN", AND IN THE CENTRE THE INITIALS OF THE HOLY FAMILY: J M J (JESUS, MARY AND JOSEPH).

← OVER THE FRONT DOOR, SURROUNDING A CYPRESS, SYMBOL OF WELCOME, APPEARS A C, INITIAL OF THE OWNERS.

→ ON THE DOORKNOCKER WE COME ACROSS A CURIOUS NATURALIST DETAIL: AN INSECT THAT IS SQUASHED BY A GREEK CROSS WHEN KNOCKING AT THE DOOR.

▶ Barcelona

Heritage Site of National Interest

Casa Figueras
Torre Bellesguard

At the beginning of the 15th century, Martin I the Humane built, at the foot of the Collserola hills, a palace which he called Bellesguard, meaning beautiful view. Five centuries later, in 1900, over the same spot, Antoni Gaudí erected a building for Maria Sagués Molins that demonstrated a peculiar neo-gothic style that pays homage to Catalan Gothic art and architecture.

▶ The name
Bellesguard, beautiful view, owes its name to the poet Bernat Metge, who named thus the bucolic setting of the marriage of the last king of the Catalan-Aragonese dynasty, due to its splendid views over Barcelona and the sea.

▶ **Torre Bellesguard** Bellesguard, 16-20. Barcelona

A detached, isolated house, with a square ground plan and 19.5 metres in height and built as a private residence. The exterior is noted for its marked cubic volume and slender angular tower.

It is structured in five levels (lower ground floor, ground floor, first floor and two lofts, the second in the form of an attic) and the inside possesses a very rich atmosphere where highly original constructive and structural solutions are applied. In this sense the stairwell of the house really stands out, the veritable backbone of the building, painted white and illuminated by a stained-glass window of intense colours that stick out towards the exterior in the form of a star.

The roofing is also notable, structurally resolved with the two levels of lofts, one as a support and the other as a coronation, built with walls, partitions and solid open brickwork arches which lighten the weight on this high part of the house. The crowning level forms the external appearance of the roof, flanked by merlons and a walkway.

The building is made in solid brick which Gaudí covered with local slate classified according to the grey, brown, yellow and green shades, recreating the Roman technique of Opus incertum, thus maintaining a dialogue with the natural setting.

The architect used a curious system to produce the speckled masonry of the facade. He started with a clay model to obtain a plaster mould, at the bottom of which he placed small stones which, on being covered with the mortar, stuck to it, thereby creating an original surface in the final piece.

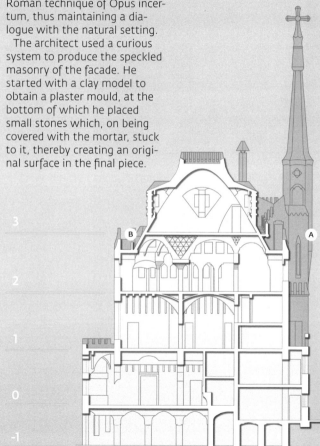

A Tower   **B** Walkway

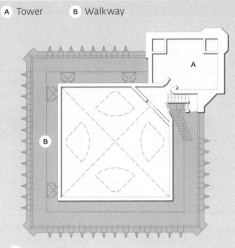

► **3** Upper attic

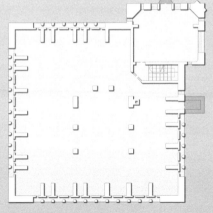

► **2** Lower attic

▷ Initials

Domènec Sugrañes, collaborator of Gaudí, designed the mosaics of the bench, although the master's hand can be made out in the F and the V of widow Figueras, the owner.

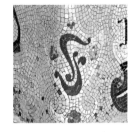

▽ Lions and roosters

The tiles of the vestibule and the stairway contain these symbols of royalty in a particular Gaudian homage to the past splendour of Catalonia.

▽ Doorknocker

The doorknocker stands out for its detailed naturalist design of osseous forms that remind one of a femur that swings from the hip joint.

▶ **Torre Bellesguard**

Tower
The ideological pro-
gramme of Bellesguard
refers to the decline of
the Catalan dynasty,
with the death (1410)
of Martin the Humane
without descendents,
and the desire of late
19th-century pro-Cata-
lan consciousness to
recover the old splen-
dour. The tower culmi-
nates in the colours of
the Catalan flag, a roy-
al crown and the four-
armed cross.

Venus
The spectacular
stained-glass window
is interpreted as Venus,
the star of the sunset,
but also of the dawn.

Catalan fish
On the benches, fish
carry the Catalan flag
and crown in reference
to the hegemony of
medieval Catalonia in
the Mediterranean.

Viaduct
Gaudí rerouted an old
path and supported it
over vaulting sustained
by inclining pillars similar to those in Park
Güell.

Coat of arms
Inside the wall (of the
few remains still stand-
ing of the king's palace)
Gaudí had the Catalan
coat of arms sculpted
alongside a sun and a
moon.

→
DESPITE BEING INSPIRED BY
THE GOTHIC STYLE, GAUDÍ
SURPASSED MERE FORMAL
IMITATION.

→
THE ROOFING OF BELLESGUARD
REMINDS ONE OF A DRAGON'S
HEAD.

P. 144-145
→
DETAIL OF THE STAINED GLASS
IN THE MAIN DOOR.

→
THE ROUGH APPEARANCE OF
THE SCHISTOSE STONE ON THE
EXTERIOR CONTRASTS WITH
THE WHITE LOBBY IN WHICH
LIGHT AND COLOUR FILTER
THROUGH THE STAINED GLASS.

P. 146-147
→
THE STRUCTURE OF ARCHES
AND FALSE ARCHES ON THE
ATTICS DEMONSTRATES THE
FUSION OF FUNCTIONALITY
AND AESTHETICISM IN
GAUDIAN ARCHITECTURE.

▶ **Barcelona**

UNESCO World Heritage Site

Park Güell

On a piece of land on the Muntanya Pelada, in the Barcelona district of La Salut, Eusebi Güell wanted to build an urbanisation inspired by the concept of the garden city. In this he sought to return to nature, health and an escape from the insalubrious industrial city. Mainly assisted by Rubió, Berenguer and Jujol, Gaudí worked on the construction of this park between 1900 and 1914, and even moved his home there in 1906.

▷ **Medallions**
The name of the park in English is explained by the influence that the British garden cities had over the genesis of Güell and Gaudí's project.

149

▶ **Park Güell** Carrer Olot and carretera del Carmel. Barcelona

A private residential urban development, never originally designed as a park, and planned in accordance with the British taste for "garden cities" (thus taking the English name park inscribed on the main entrance).

Gaudí partially developed the 15 hectares of land in the district of La Salut in Gràcia, in the northern part of the city, in an area known as the Muntanya Pelada (the bald mountain), rather rocky and full of slopes. Gaudí designed all the necessary services for the community, with a project that encompassed seventy sites with gardens, building viaducts, squares and streets, closure walls and porters' lodges, as well as a large entrance stairway and a hypostyle hall for a covered market. Over this is a large public square, bordered by a winding bench built from ergonomically designed prefabricated modules.

The square is a collecting point for rainwater, which is channelled through the columns and taken to a tank below the hypostyle hall, where it is stored to be used for watering.

An outstanding feature of Park Güell is the integration of architecture with nature, the two concepts always in total harmony. In order to save the natural slopes, Gaudí built viaducts from brick pillars, which he covered with stone obtained from the excavations. He also thought about the vegetation, respecting the existing plantlife and planting new species in the park, such as carob trees, palm trees, wisteria and rosemary.

▶ Porter's pavilion

A Reception

B Park Güell Information Centre

C Chimneys

D Cross

▶ Keeper's house pavillon

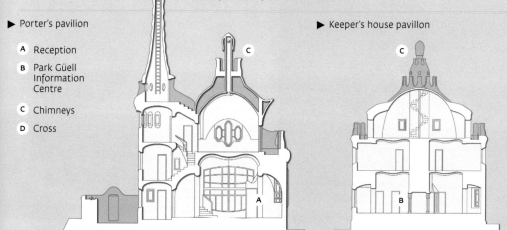

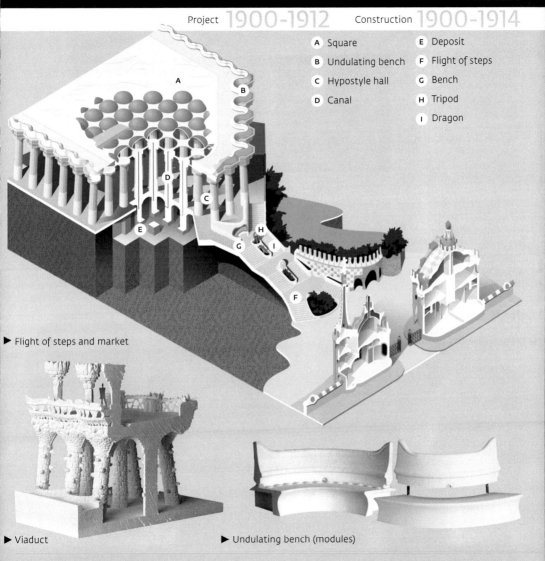

Project 1900-1912   Construction 1900-1914

A Square
B Undulating bench
C Hypostyle hall
D Canal

E Deposit
F Flight of steps
G Bench
H Tripod
I Dragon

▶ Flight of steps and market

▶ Viaduct

▶ Undulating bench (modules)

▶ Park Güell

Coffee cups

The effect of the white scales of the *Amanita muscaria* that crowns the Keeper's house pavillon was down to Gaudí's use of inverted coffee cups.

Warped surfaces

Difficult to decorate, Gaudí achieved it with the *trencadís* technique, mosaic of pieces of ceramic previously broken into small pieces.

Stone omphalus

Situated inside a curious trípod that culminates the stairway, it may refer to what overlooked the oracle of the sanctuary of Apollo in Delphos.

Dragon

In the original font, the dragon's appearance was fiercer than the current one, since the paws and the teeth were much more noticeable.

Coat of arms of Nimes

The dragon of the stairway and the palm tree of the garden of Güell's house recall the period as student of the count in Nimes.

Tower

The chequered white and blue of the hyberboloid of external undulating faces culminates in a type of metallic spout crowned by the four-armed cross.

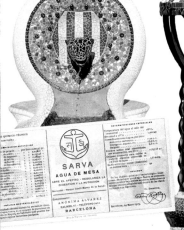

Health

The snake and eucalyptus fruits are symbols of medicine and health, like the medicinal mineral water found in the park and which the name of SARVA was commercialised by Güell.

Interior

Gaudí dealt with the humbler spaces with great care and variety of resources, as can be seen in this pavilion.

Graffiti

Jujol and Gaudí carved simple Marian invocations onto the knee-high pieces of the bench, and other more mysterious ones, with varied graphics.

▶ **Park Güell**

Washerwoman

Popular tradition has seen in this figure a washerwoman with her basket of clothes over her head and the stick to beat the clothes (now disappeared) in her right hand.

Living stone

These flowerpots, covered with stone from the site, have a rough and fragile beauty that seems to emerge from the land itself.

The three crosses

Above an atavistic structure, Gaudí placed three rather unconventional crosses. That of Jesus and that of the good thief were crowned by a pyramid, and the third is an arrow.

 Suns

The four soffits on the ceiling of the colonnade share a single design in the form of sun, although with variations of colour and materials, such as this doll.

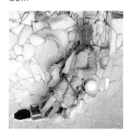

Cistern

Beneath the colonnade and via the hollow shaft of some columns, which channel the rainwater that falls on the square, the cistern, which was built from pilasters that support simple stone vaulting, fills. The overflow is, in fact, the mouth of the dragon on the stairway.

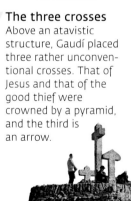

P. 155
←
THE DORIC COLONNADE
WHICH SUPPORTS THE SQUARE
IS AN IMPOSING SPACE THAT,
PARADOXICALLY, WAS
DESIGNED AS A MARKETPLACE.

→
BETWEEN 1900 AND 1903
THE MAIN BUILDINGS OF PARK
GÜELL WERE CONSTRUCTED:
WALLS, THE MAIN STAIRWAY,
PAVILIONS, ETC.
THE PAVILIONS STAND OUT FOR
THEIR IMAGINATIVE, LYRICAL
AND CHROMATIC NATURE, AS
WELL AS THE EXPRESSIVENESS
OF ELEMENTS SUCH AS THE
TOWER CROWNED BY
THE FOUR-ARMED CROSS.
→
CENTRAL COLUMN OF THE
CARRIAGE SHELTER. IT HAS THE
FORM OF A GLASS AND IS
INSPIRED BY SOME
ROMANESQUE CRYPTS.

→
GENERAL VIEW OF THE BENCH
AND COLONNADE TOGETHER.
→
ON THE STEPS, WE COME
ACROSS NOT ONLY THE
SALAMANDER BUT ALSO
ORNAMENTS SUCH AS THE
MEDALLION WITH THE COAT OF
ARMS OF CATALONIA FROM
WHICH PROJECTS A SPOUT IN
THE SHAPE OF A SNAKE'S HEAD.

P. 160-161
→
THE SALAMANDER,
A LEGENDARY ANIMAL
CHARGED WITH SYMBOLISM,
IS THE OUTLET FOR THE
TANK SITUATED BELOW
THE COLONNADE.
→
DETAIL OF THE BACK
OF THE SALAMANDER.

→
THE CEILING ROSES OF THE
COLONNADE, ATTRIBUTED
TO JUJOL, SHOW COLOURIST
INTERPRETATIONS OF SUNS,
MEDUSAS, ETC.

P. 164-165
→→
THE CURVE IN MOVEMENT
AND THE SNAKING
UNDULATION DOMINATE THE
ARCHITECTURAL RHYTHM OF
PARK GÜELL, REACHING ITS
MAXIMUM EXPRESSION IN THE
SNAKE-LIKE BENCH AROUND
THE SQUARE.

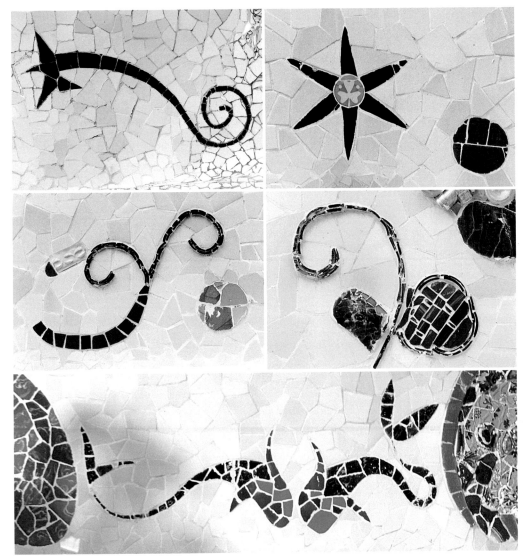

P. 166-167

←

THE BENCH IS DECORATED
WITH ABSTRACT
COMPOSITIONS COEVAL WITH
THE FIRST NON-FIGURATIVE
PAINTINGS OF KANDINSKY.

←

DETAILS OF THE BIOMORPHIC
DECORATION OF THE BENCH.

→

FRANCESC BERENGUER, ONE
OF GAUDÍ'S COLLABORATORS,
BUILT THIS HOUSE BETWEEN
1903 AND 1904 AS A MODEL FOR
THE CHALETS THAT WERE TO BE
BUILT IN PARK GÜELL. GAUDÍ
LIVED IN IT FROM 1906 AND
TODAY IT IS THE MUSEUM
DEDICATED TO THE ARCHITECT.

→

THE PORTICOES OF LEANING
COLUMNS CONTRAST THEIR
DRAMATIC TAWNY COLOUR
WITH THE CHROMATISM OF
THE REST OF THE PARK.

▶ **Palma, Mallorca**

Cathedral of Mallorca

In 1901, Pere Campins Barceló, the bishop of Majorca, entrusted Gaudí to restore the cathedral. The works lasted for a total of ten years (1904–1914) and they were surrounded by constant controversy that resulted finally in Gaudí's dismissal after the death of Campins. Basically, the reform work involved recovering the space occupied by a Gothic-renaissance choir situated in the centre of the nave. Also collaborating on the restoration work were, among others, Joan Rubió Bellver, Vicente Villarrubias, Torres García and Josep Maria Jujol.

▷ **Innovation**

Gaudí developed his own system ("trichomy") of stained-glass window construction, using three sheets of glass to obtain the desired colour and a fourth piece in matt to tone it down.

▶ **Cathedral of Mallorca**

In 1901, Pere Joan Campins commissioned Gaudí to restore the Cathedral of Mallorca. The architect presented a project in which he proposed the following reforms: take down the altar-pieces to free the space of the presbytery and place the choir there, which was in the centre of the nave; place new pulpits, place a baldaquin over the main altar, open the blind Gothic windows, decorate the cathedral with furniture and paintings, and open the chapel to place the tombs of Jaume II and Jaume III of Mallorca. In 1903, the canons gave their approval of the proposed reforms and the architect moved to Mallorca with his collaborators.

One of the most interesting interventions was the replacement of the old stained-glass windows with primary colours which, one behind another and lit up by the sun, produce the secondary colours providing the desired effect by means of varied gradations. These stained-glass windows, designed by Torres i Garcia, are attributed to the leading Barcelona firms of Hijos de E. R. Amigó and Rigalt, Granell y Cía.

The times when Gaudí and his collaborators stayed in Mallorca are accompanied by many anecdotes, among which feature the incident that Jujol provoked on painting the choir stalls. He painted "La sang d'Ell sobre nosaltres" [His blood over us] on them. The canons took it personally and felt insulted and immediately after the death of Bishop Campins, Gaudí's main defender, they made the architect leave the work.

Despite everything, this reform was considered as being a veritable revitalisation of the cathedral, both in terms of recovering spaces and in the renewal of its liturgical meaning. This is shown in a letter dated 1909 by the priest Miquel Costa i Llobera where he wrote, "Gaudí, restoring the See of Mallorca, has revealed the entire meaning of its theological sense".

The tintinabulum

A small bell that announces the arrival of the procession of the clergy of the basilica was designed by Gaudí along with 11 other pieces of liturgical furnishing.

Electric light

In this candelabra-tiara of the Trinity, as well as in another four and in 12 candelabras, Gaudí introduced electric lighting in the cathedral.

Stained-glass windows

Of an almost expressionist aesthetic, these unfinished fragments destined for the royal chapel are on display in the chapel of Saint Bernard.

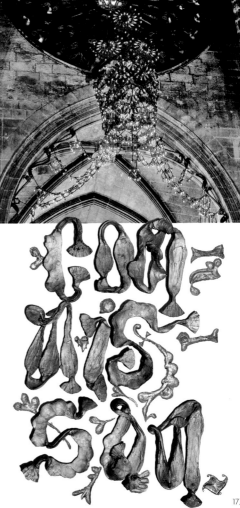

The stairway

It is the most sumptuous furnishing and is used for the display of the Holy Sacrament in the main altar.

Gilded letters

For the Episcopal chair, Gaudí and Jujol designed some gilded letters in wrought iron that refer, in Latin, to the ordination of the bishops.

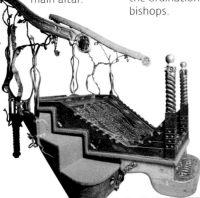

→
REPRESENTATION OF
BRANCHES AND EPISCOPAL
COATS OF ARMS.
→
PAINTINGS BY JOSEP MARIA
JUJOL OVER THE CHOIR STALL.

▶ **Barcelona**

UNESCO World Heritage Site

Casa Batlló

Between 1904 and 1907, Antoni Gaudí worked for the industrialist Josep Batlló Casanovas reforming a house built in 1877 and located in Passeig de Gràcia in Barcelona. The decoration of the house, on which he was assisted by Josep Maria Jujol, expresses a fully-fledged modernist language. Nevertheless, the Barcelona population of the period were quite astonished by this work and quickly gave it nicknames such as the "house of bones" or the "house of yawns".

▶ **Ceramic discs**
With the traditional technique of firing the clay and natural oxide enamels, Gaudí achieves a façade of texture and aesthetics that refer to pictorial impressionism.

► **Casa Batlló** Passeig de Gràcia, 43. Barcelona

Reform and modernisation of a commercial and residential building between party walls. It is one of the most radical interventions made by Gaudí, who did not hesitate in remaking the entire main facade of the old building, with fluid forms, sinuous undulations and an elaborate vitreous trencadís skin that shines with differing intensity according to the position of the sun.

The property is made up of seven floors (basement, ground floor, first floor, four more floors and the attics). On the first floor, also called the main floor and built as the owner's home, he projected an enormous gallery with highly expressive osseous and naturalist forms, in which he included a large sash window with an ingenious system that enabled it to be opened fully to the outside. The home is entered by a sumptuous, independent stairway, closed off from the other residents. It is worth noting the special attention given to the Batlló family home, for which Gaudí invented devices that would provide more inner light and ventilation, built the famous curved and unending ceilings and walls and designed the private chapel of the house

and all the furniture, from the doors to the tables, chairs and stools.

Gaudí also modified the inner courtyards of the old building and widened them with the aim of letting air and light pass through, which is filtered down to the ground floor by a large central skylight. The gradation of colour in the inner courtyard goes from deep blue at the top down to white at the bottom, and the size of the windows, which get larger in the lower floors, are the result of Gaudí's desire to control the entry of light into the building.

Gaudí also reformed the rear facade, on which he placed large balconies and once again embellished with trencadís, covered with differently coloured ceramic scales, to which he added a bulbous-shaped tower culminating in a four-armed cross, decorated with the anagrams of the Sagrada Família.

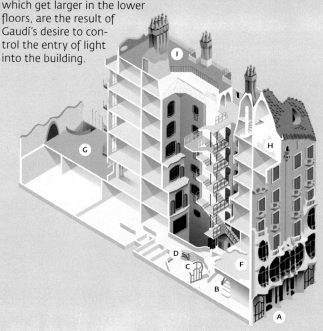

Project: October **1904**   Construction **1904-1907**

- **A** Entrance
- **B** Resident's stairway
- **C** First floor stairway
- **D** Lift
- **E** Fire place
- **F** Gallery
- **G** Rear courtyard
- **H** Loft
- **I** Flat roof

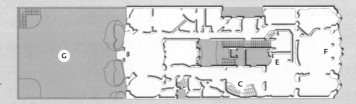

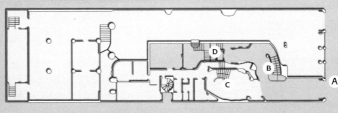

▶ **1** Main floor

▶ **0** Ground floor

Passeig de Gràcia

▶ **Casa Batlló** Passeig de Gràcia 43, Barcelona

▷ Upright

On the handrail of the private stairway, the upright recalls the solidified splash of a drop of water or the crown that tops a sceptre.

Bulbous cross

The four-armed cross is this time raised over a bulbous base, which emphasises the organic nature of the building, on a tower –conceived to be in the centre– that Gaudí moved to the side in order not to break brusquely with the adjoining building.

Tibias

The thin columns of the galleries are tibias from which begin to sprout the plant life as a symbol of death but also of life and regeneration.

Ironwork

The ironwork of the doors (handles, latches, doorknockers…) were designed by Gaudí moulding their forms in clay before making them in tin.

▽ The Holy Family

In the oratory, Gaudí installed this soffit by the sculptor Josep Llimona. Today it can be seen in the museum of the Sagrada Família.

◁ Flooring

Although it was designed for the Casa Batlló, this flooring of hexagonal floor tiles with decoration of marine elements was placed in the Casa Milà.

Soft matter

In the ergonomic design by Gaudí –it is said that the architect used his workers to obtain these forms on soft clay– the oak wood of which the chairs and seats are made seem to have lost their compactness, their solidity, as if they had lost their very qualities of wood.

→

THE CASA BATLLÓ REPRESENTS
A NEW ARCHITECTURAL
EXPRESSION IN WHICH
REFERENCES TO HISTORICAL
STYLES HAVE BEEN SURPASSED.
THE FACADE IS COVERED WITH
CERAMIC DISCS AND
COLOURED GLASS WINDOWS.

→

ON THE LOWER PART OF THE
MAIN FACADE, SANDSTONE
FROM MONTJUÏC WAS
SCULPTED INTO SINUOUS
FORMS.

P. 184-185

→

DETAIL OF ONE OF THE
CERAMIC DISCS OF THE FAÇADE.

→

THE RAILINGS OF THE
BALCONIES OF THE FAÇADE ARE
CAST IRON AND PAINTED IVORY
AND GOLD. THEY LOOK LIKE
MASKS OR MAY REMIND ONE
OF A SKULL

← GENERAL STAIRWAY OF THE BUILDING .

← THE STRUCTURAL HARMONY COMBINED WITH THE AESTHETIC EFFECT CREATE SUGGESTIVE INTERIORS THAT ARE FILLED WITH DETAIL. THE DOORS ON THE MAIN STAIRWAY ARE DECORATED WITH CARVED SHAPES IN RELIEF THAT ARE LIKE BONES.

P. 188-189
→→
GAUDÍ ENLARGED THE STAIRWELL AND DECORATED IT BRILLIANTLY WITH A LAYER OF CERAMIC USING FLAT PIECES AND OTHERS IN RELIEF THAT HE DESIGNED HIMSELF. BENEATH THE SKYLIGHT THEY ARE COBALT BLUE AND AS THEY DESCEND AND MOVE FURTHER AWAY FROM THE ENTRANCE OF LIGHT THEY BECOME BLUE, SKY BLUE, PEARL GREY AND WHITE, CREATING ONE OF THE MOST SURPRISING CHROMATIC PLAYS OF LIGHT BY THE ARCHITECT, SINCE IF ONE LOOKS UP FROM THE WELL, THE IMPRESSION IS THAT THE COLOUR IS PRACTICALLY UNIFORM.

←←
REGARDING THE LIGHT THAT
CAN BE CAPTURED, THE
WINDOWS ARE LARGER ON THE
LOWER FLOORS AND DECREASE
IN SIZE HIGHER UP. THIS
CREATES AN IMPRESSION OF
ACCELERATION OF PERSPECTIVE
WHEN THE WELL IS SEEN FROM
BELOW AND AVOIDS THE
SENSATION OF A DEEP WELL
WHEN SEEN FROM ABOVE.

P. 192-193
→→
PRIVATE ACCESS STAIRWAY TO
THE MAIN FLOOR. IT IS MADE
OF OAK AND THE CARVED
PIECES OF THE CROWNING OF
THE STEPS SUCCEED EACH
OTHER LIKE VERTEBRAE OF THE
BACKBONE OF A DRAGON
INSIDE A CAVE

P. 194-195
→
THE CHIMNEY –EMBEDDED
INTO THE WALL IN THE STYLE
OF CATALAN COUNTRY
HOUSES– IS AN EXAMPLE OF
THE PERFECT FUSION BETWEEN
DESIGN AND FUNCTIONALITY.
→
ON THE MAIN FLOOR, THE
DESIGN OF THE FURNISHING
AND CABINETWORK
DEMONSTRATE GAUDÍ'S
CONCERN FOR DETAIL. THE
GLASS PASTE DISCS ON THE
DOORS REMIND ONE OF THE
COLOURING ON THE FACADE.

→
THE MAIN ROOMS OPEN TO
THE STREET BY MEANS OF
STAINED-GLASS WINDOWS
DECORATED WITH SIBAS, THE
COLOURED VITREOUS PASTE
DISCS.

→
THE CEILING OF THE CENTRAL
ROOM IS A FLAT SKY THAT
FORMS A WHIRLPOOL WHICH,
AS WELL AS CONSTITUTING
ANOTHER MARINE
REFERENCES, REFERS, AS IS
COMMON WITH GAUDÍ, TO THE
IDEA OF GENERATION OF
NATURE.

P. 198-199
→
THE REAR FAÇADE IS
ORGANISED BY MEANS OF THE
SUPERPOSITION OF
CONTINUOUS BALCONIES TO
WHICH WIDE FRENCH
WINDOWS OPEN OUT. THE
RAILING OF THESE BALCONIES
ARE MADE UP OF VERY
TRANSPARENT IRON GRILLES,
GIVING OFF A SENSATION OF
GREAT LIGHTNESS.

→
THE COURTYARD IS DECORATED
WITH PEBBLES AND FLOWER
BOXES COVERED WITH
CERAMIC DISCS AND GLASS
AND CERAMIC TRENCADÍS OF
DIFFERENT COLOURS WITH
DARK GREENS DOMINATING.

←→
THE LOFT IS BUILT BY MEANS
OF PARTITIONED VAULTS OF
A PARABOLIC SECTION,
PLASTERED AND PAINTED
WHITE. IT SURROUNDS THE
WELL AND WAS USED AS A
STORAGE ROOM, WASHROOMS
AND A PLACE FOR HANGING
THE CLOTHES TO DRY.

→
THE CERAMIC OF A BULBOUS
FORM THAT SUPPORTS THE
FOUR-ARMED CROSS COMES
FROM MALLORCA AND IN THE
TOWER THAT SUPPORTS IT
THERE ARE, IN A SPIRAL, THREE
MONOGRAMS OF JESUS (JHS),
JOSEPH (JHP) AND MARY (M),
THE HOLY FAMILY.

→
ON THE ROOF, THE
SCULPTURAL TREATMENT
OF THE CHIMNEYS AND THEIR
COVERING WITH CERAMIC AND
PAINTED GLASS SHOW US
GAUDÍ AT HIS MOST
COLOURIST, PERHAPS DUE TO
HIS COLLABORATION WITH
JUJOL.

P. 204-205
→
THE "SCALES" OF THE ROOF ARE
THE WORK OF PUJOL & BAUCIS.

→
THE ROOFING IS CROWNED IN
THE FORM OF A BACKBONE BY
CERAMIC PIECES THAT
ALTERNATE BETWEEN
CYLINDRICAL AND SPHERICAL
SHAPES.

▶ Barcelona

Heritage Site of National Interest
UNESCO World Heritage Site

Casa Milà
La Pedrera

The widow Roser Segimon, heir to a vast fortune amassed by her first husband in the American colonies, was remarried to Pere Milà, an important Barcelona businessman. This wealthy couple wanted to build a building in Passeig de Gràcia and so they hired the most expensive and famous architect: Antoni Gaudí. The construction, which took from 1906 until 1912, resulted in a monumental building, but also caused disagreements between Gaudí and the Milà family. The Casa Milà was the architect's last piece of civil engineering.

▶ **Mystical rose**

Just above the rose with the M of Mary that is on the high part of the façade, Gaudí wanted to place a sculpture of the Virgin of 4.5 m which Milà vehemently rejected.

▶ **La Pedrera** Passeig de Gràcia, 92. Barcelona

A huge residential building that was soon baptised by the Barcelona public as the La Pedrera, or stone quarry, due to its rocky outside appearance. Built in a mould-breaking architectural language, Gaudí did not finish the final stage of the project because of the differences he had with the owners.

The architect occupied a site of 1,620 m², over which he built on 1,323 m² as an undulating curve, both on the outside and the inside of the building, applying multiple solutions of controlled geometry as well as elements of a naturalist nature. In reality, the building is made up of two estates (with independent entrances but joined by the same facade), and although each has a central courtyard, the owners' home covered the total surface area of the two.

Unlike the Casa Calvet and the Casa Batlló, the Casa Milà has a structure of stone, solid brick and metallic beams that release the facade from the load-bearing functions and permit large openings for light and air to enter. This original feature, totally new compared to the traditional master walls, means that even today any partition

can be knocked down without affecting the building's solidity, in an architectural precedent similar to that which some years later Le Corbusier would call "free plan". With the pillar system Gaudí was able to give different uses to the nine levels of the house. The basement was a garage for cars (the first underground car park in the city), the ground floor was for commercial establishments, the mezzanine for offices, the first floor the owners' home, the four upper floors for rent and the loft and attic for the laundry.

Over the latter part, configured by a series of walled up brick parabolic arches, Gaudí built the attic rooftop from which stand out amazing chimneys, ventilators and stairway exits of almost sculptural proportions. The rest of the building is also notable for the way in which it is resolved: the curious iron structure supporting the circular courtyard, the wide vestibules, the wrought iron balconies, the

smooth plasterwork ceilings with dynamic relief work, the woodwork on the doors, windows and furniture, the design of the knobs, handles and peepholes, as well as a hydraulic flooring (originally designed for the Casa Batlló) of a hexagonal shape that Barcelona City Council took as a model to cover the pavements of Passeig de Gràcia.

In 1986 the Casa Milà, one of the symbols of Barcelona, was bought by the Caixa Catalunya financial entity, who, after restoring it, set up a space for temporary exhibitions and one permanent one: the Espai Gaudí.

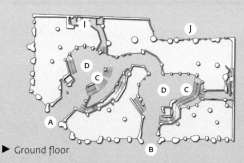

▶ Ground floor

Project: February 1906   Construction 1906–1912

A Entrance Passeig de Gràcia

B Entrance Carrer Provença

C Steps

D Vestibule

E Main floor

F Espai Gaudí loft

G Walkway

H Terrace

I Resident's stairway

J Rear façade

Passeig de Gràcia

Carrer Provença

▶ Main floor

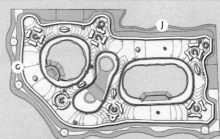

▶ H Terrace

▶ La Pedrera

▶ **Sculptural group**
This drawing by Joan Matamala shows the sculpture by Carles Mani that should have crowned the façade and which the owner refused to place on it (in 1909 there had been an uprising in the city and 80 religious buildings were burnt).

▲ **Mask and bird**
Although the railings of the balconies are an extraordinary piece of work of abstract forms (pages 216-218), some details are figurative.

The columns of the residential floor of the Milà family contain numerous reliefs and inscriptions, such as this cross in a whirlpool (right) or the dove on the left.

On the columns of the residential floor appear some mysterious inscriptions in Catalan, such as *Oblida* (forgetfulness) or *Perdona* (forgiveness).

Symbols of innocence, and also of Saint Joseph, husband of the Virgin Mary, these lilies are found at the top of the façade, to the left of the inscriptions.

Ave Gratia Plena Dominus Tecum is the phrase that crowns the façade and where the rose with the M replaces the word Mary.

▶ **La Pedrera**

Doors
The marks or traces in the wrought iron of the vestibule doors give the iron the quality of something soft worked by the hand of man.

Chimneys
The most popular figures of the Pedrera, they seem like silent guardians that the erosion of the wind and rain has sculpted in the rock.

Heart
In the warriors-chimney there are enigmatic signs that emphasise their disturbing appearance and other more recognisable ones, such as this Heart of Jesus.

Grilles
On giving the elements of the grilles a winding movement like silk ribbons, Gaudí gives the sensation of lightness to a heavy material.

Vestibule
The colouring of the mural paintings along with the effect of the light that penetrates from the courtyard increases the sensation of an underwater cave.

→
GALLERY ON THE FIRST FLOOR
OF LA PEDRERA.

→
THE IMPOSING UNDULATING
FACADE OF LA PEDRERA
SUGGESTS THE LIFE AND
MOVEMENT OF THE STONE.

P. 216-217
→→
THE RAILS ON THE BALCONIES,
AUTHENTIC IRON SCULPTURES,
WERE CREATED BY JUJOL USING
THE FIRST ONE AS A MODEL,
WHICH WAS DESIGNED AND
EVEN CAST BY GAUDÍ HIMSELF.

P. 218-219
→
THE CAST IRON DOORS
COVER THE ENTRANCE LIKE
SPIDERS' WEBS.

→
THE STRUCTURE OF LA
PEDRERA IS OPEN PLAN, AN
ARCHITECTURAL SOLUTION
WITH WHICH THE BUILDING IS
SUPPORTED BY COLUMNS,
FREEING THE FACADES FROM
THE LOAD.

THE IMPORTANCE THAT GAUDÍ GIVES TO THE COURTYARDS AS DISTRIBUTORS OF LIGHT AND VENTILATION REACHES ITS ZENITH IN THE PEDRERA ON TURNING THEM INTO AUTHENTIC INTERIOR FAÇADES, DUE TO BOTH THEIR DIMENSIONS AND ARCHITECTURAL TREATMENT.

P. 222-223
→
ON THE GRILLES OF THE BALCONIES THE ART OF WROUGHT IRON WORK ACHIEVES A SURPRISING STYLISTIC TREATMENT.
→
THE SENSATION OF MOVEMENT OF MILÀ'S FLAT IS ENHANCED BY CEILINGS THAT IMITATE THE SURFACE OF A SEA, WITH WHIRLPOOLS AND WAVES SEEN FROM THEIR DEPTHS.

P. 224-225
→
THE FLAT ROOF SEEMS TO SOFTEN AND MELT INTO THE WALLS OF THE LOFT OVER THE GAP OF THE INNER COURTYARD.
→
COURTYARD OF THE VESTIBULE OF PASSEIG DE GRÀCIA. IN THE INITIAL PROJECT, GAUDÍ THOUGHT ABOUT THE POSSIBILITY OF CREATING A SPIRAL RAMP THAT WOULD ENABLE CARS TO REACH AS FAR AS THE LANDING OF EACH FLOOR.

→

THE LOFT IS ONE OF THE
MOST EXTRAORDINARY SPACES
CREATED BY GAUDÍ, A SERIES
OF 270 PARTITIONED ARCHES IN
CATENARY FORM AND
DIFFERENT HEIGHTS IN AN
UNDULATING AND WINDING
SEQUENCE. AS IN CASA BATLLÓ,
ITS FUNCTION WAS
WASHROOM AND DRYING
SPACE.

→→
THE BUILDING'S ROOF
RECREATES AN ONEIRIC AND
SUGGESTIVE WORLD WHERE
CHIMNEYS AND VENTILATION
DUCTS ARE TRANSFORMED
INTO DISTURBING
ANTHROMORPHIC SHAPES.

P. 230-231
→
THE FLAT ROOF OF LA PEDRERA
SYNTHESISES AND PERFECTS
THE TREATMENT THAT GAUDÍ
GAVE TO ALL THE CROWNING
ELEMENTS THROUGHOUT
THE WORK.

▶ Santa Coloma de Cervelló, Catalonia

Heritage Site of National Interest
UNESCO World Heritage Site

Crypt of the Güell Industrial Village

Eusebi Güell established an industrial village in Santa Coloma de Cervelló (Barcelona). Here, Gaudí had to build a new church of which he was only able to complete then crypt. The architect, who had started the project in 1898, abandoned the direction of the works in 1914. The piece as a whole is, possibly, Gaudí's master work, and here he could test architectural solutions that he would later use in the Sagrada Família.

▷ **Crosses and flowers**
The leaded stained-glass windows draw large crosses, each one a different design, based on flower petals.

▶ **Crypt of the Güell Industrial Village** Colònia Güell. Santa Coloma de Cervelló

A building devoted to worship for the workers of the Güell Industrial Village (Santa Coloma de Cervelló, Barcelona) from which it takes its name.

The portico is formed by a forest of leaning columns of basalt stone and brick that maintain an intimate dialogue with the surrounding landscape, made up mainly of pine trees. The columns support polygonal arches whose guidelines form a series of convex vaults of hyperbolic paraboloids that Gaudí decorated with ceramics in the shape of a cross. The crypt is reached by passing through the portico. It has a starred polygonal ground plan and pillars of brick, basalt or limestone, according to the loads they have to withstand.

The walls are covered with vitrified slag that came from the waste of the smelting furnaces, and the grilles of the large windows were made from recycled sewing machine needles. Everything, along with the trencadís mosaic, emphasises the idea of providing the humblest of materials with dignity.

Another remarkable aspect of the crypt is the abundant Christian iconography it contains: fish, the letters alpha and omega, which signify the beginning and the end, crosses, monograms of Christ, St. Andrew's crosses, etc.

For the interior, Gaudí designed the church pews and several stained-glass windows in suggestive chromatic shades, while Josep Maria Jujol was entrusted with the central altar. All these elements disappeared in 1936, when the crypt was ransacked and damaged, losing a part of the pews (reproduced in 1960), the stained-glass windows (restored in 1980) and the central altar (redesigned by Peter Harden in 1965).

Complete model of the project for the church at the Colònia. © Museu Diocesà – Gaudí Exhibition Centre

▶ Crypt

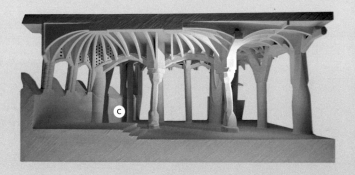

A Porch

B Entrance

C Altar

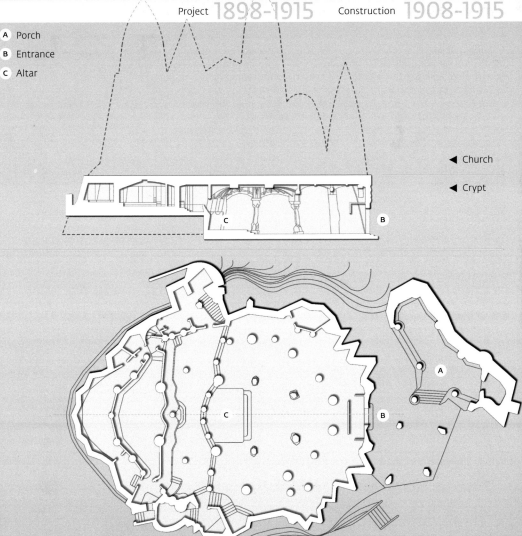

◄ Church

◄ Crypt

▶ Crypt of the Güell Industrial Village

The Holy Family
One of the keystones set into the portico vaulting is decorated with the anagram of the Holy Family: the M of Mary, the saw of Saint Joseph and the cross of Jesus.

Temperance
The mosaic of the cardinal virtues is found above the door. In this case temperance, a typical jug for drinking wine, very popular among Catalan workers.

Recycling
The grilles protecting the windows are formed by needles of looms from the colony that are threaded to form hexagons with stars in the centre, a figure much loved by Gaudí, who used it in nearly all his works as a symbol of industry and community.

Holy water
The fonts of holy water, as in the Sagrada Família, are large seashells supported on wrought iron structures.

Church pews
Unlike his earlier choir stalls, Gaudí designed the pews for this church combining wood and iron.

Christian symbolism
In the portico, an infinite number of *trencadís* mosaics are Christian symbols: the Alpha and Omega (God the beginning and end of all things), the fish (secret symbol under the Roman Empire), the staurogram, the earliest symbol of Jesus on the cross, etc.

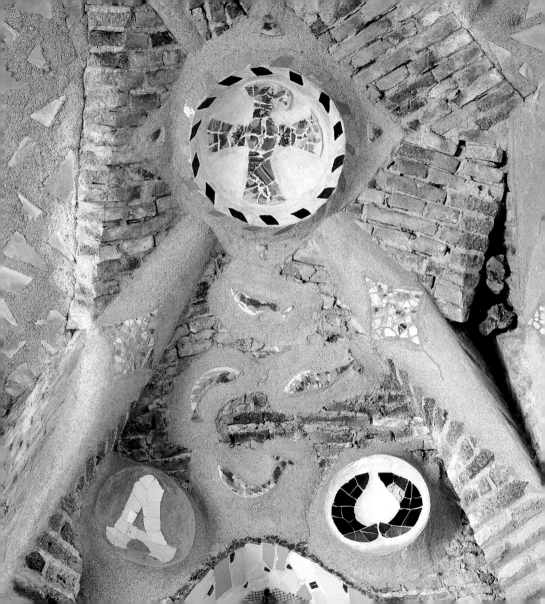

→
THE ARCHITECTURE
HARMONISES WITH THE
NATURAL ENVIRONMENT THAT
GAUDÍ RESPECTED, EVEN
CHANGING THE SHAPE OF THE
STAIRWAY IN ORDER TO SAVE A
TREE: "I CAN MAKE A STAIRWAY
IN 3 WEEKS BUT IT TAKES
20 YEARS TO MAKE A PINE
TREE".

→
THE CRYPT HAS LARGE
WINDOWS IN IRREGULAR
SHAPES, ALMOST ALL OF THEM
WITH DUST COVERS, BRICKS
ARRANGED IN AN IRREGULAR
WAY AND DARK STONES THAT
COVER THE FAÇADE. TOGETHER
IT GIVES THE WHOLE A RUSTIC
ASPECT THAT INTEGRATES
EASILY INTO THE SETTING

P. 240-241
→→
THE CRYPT IS CHARACTERISED
BY THE HYPERBOLOID ROOF,
THE PARABOLIC ARCHES AND
THE CATALAN-STYLE VAULTING.
IN THE PICTURE, THE
MONOGRAM OF CHRIST.

→
STAUROGRAM OVER THE SUN
ABOVE THE LARGE WINDOW.
  →
THE CURRENT STAINED-GLASS
WINDOWS, WHOSE FORM IS
REMINISCENT OF FLOWER
PETALS OR BUTTERFLY WINGS,
ARE A COPY OF THE ORIGINALS
THAT WERE DESTROYED IN 1936.

Other works and projects

First Mystery of Glory (1903) in the Monumental Rosary of Montserrat.

Drawing by Joan Matamala that recreates a commission that two North Americans, according to Matamala himself, gave to Gaudí to build a hotel in New York.

Door of the Miralles estate produced in 1902.

Stalls of the Sala Mercè (1904) in a photograph from the private collection en of Antoni González Moreno-Navarro. This hall, today disappeared, was one of the first cinemas in Barcelona.

Bridge in the Artigas gardens (1902) situated in the mountainous area of La Pobla de Lillet. They were created by workers from Park Güell and were not identified as a work by Gaudí until 1973.

Chalet Catllaràs, a building in the Pyrenees that Gaudí produced in 1905.

The final years (1914–1926)

In the Nerja cave (Málaga), the guide shows visitors an inverted "Sagrada Família" that hangs from the ceiling. They are Gaudí's catenaries, something the guide is not aware of. What he is also unaware of is that in the Sagrada Família, particularly on the portal of the Nativity, with its four spire bell towers, although the form is very important, it is not the most important aspect. Neither is the fact that it is integrated into nature and the architecture "lives" within the geological aspect of the work. What overshadows all this is the feeling of supernatural grandeur that invigorates each stone and which makes Gaudí not only a prodigious "inventor" within 20th-century art styles, but also the last cathedral builder, the genius who closed, not so much a period in time, but more an entire world, a world whose beginnings we were unable to chart from this or that Gothic or Romanesque cathedral but, for its virgin power, perhaps, can be dated

Flora and fauna –in this case lilies and dragonfly– on the Nativity Façade of the Sagrada Família

in the megalithic ring at Stonehenge. The texture, matter, form, light, reality and movement in Gaudí's Sagrada Família speak of a struggle and a triumph which can really not be explained, as has been said before, without referring to the supernatural. If the human power of sublimation and transformation has ever been seen in a given world in rising ascendancy —made from raw material— then it is in the Sagrada Família. The crypt is quite extraordinary with its solution of the apse pinnacles, as is the highly interesting ornamentation on the facade of the Nativity, with its peculiar softened underwater Baroque, a polyform of abstractions converted into voluminous space, of impulses transformed into shapes and with naturalistic inserts (plaster living sculptures hollowed out). None of these aspects can be compared, in our opinion, with the mystical and magical terrifying violence that the group of four parabolic bell towers possesses. These penetrative towers, simultaneously reaching to and being pulled towards the heavens represent the overcoming of a worldly human existence. The same polychrome at the tops, which we have mentioned before, is not superior to the dry harshness and stony texture of the towers that gradually thin out, making us climb with their own impetus. It is understood that Gaudí, who discovered, precisely on the project for this portal, the secret of its most prized shape and its perfect structure, wanted to devote himself entirely to this work in the twelve years before his death, before a fatal accident put an end to something that was never finished.

This feeling of infinity, more than that of being unfinished, reigns over the total creation of the Sagrada Família, particularly in the concept of its whole —loaded with the complex symbolism of the "temple-mountain" and of the "cavern"—. The model of the temple, the projects drawn by Gaudí, with the solutions for the roofing, as well as the models of specific elements, such as the elliptical windows inserted into triangles or in bony crystallisations, are the demonstration of a spirit which, instead of feeling fear from this infinity, was in fact in its true element. For Gaudí, the Sagrada Família represented the passing of Gothic architecture, not only for the elimination of the flying buttresses and buttresses or for the metamorphosis of its "ornamental structures", but also for the total conversion of its entire system, creating a new geometry, eliminating to a large extent that which was discontinuous or making the discontinuous into a continuous effect —as is seen by the simple comparison between a bell tower of the temple with gothic spires—. He was thus able to, with an irrefutable intensification of the irrational, or rather, of the super-rational, achieve what had seemed impossible to further: the ascendant rising that is judged as the essence of Faustian-Gothic. The work described in drawings by Gaudí, the unfinished work, like an immense score that no orchestra on earth would have been capable of performing, could be an enigma for future generations concerning its completion. Alternatively, it could be judged as perfectly well defined and without problems. Nevertheless, whatever the case, it is one of the architect's richest, most subtle and powerful manifestations which brought down the "traditional" system in the dawning of a world which, for its selfsame differential feeling, was forced to understand him and give him the credit that his own period unjustly and unwholesomely negated to a large extent.

To say before Gaudí's work that he was a genius of expression but question whether this quality helped him as an architect; to list, in going against such an adverse thesis, that he was the first European constructor to understand the possibilities of reinforced concrete; to say that he was the precursor of garden city urban planning; that he created, with his increased appreciation of a craftsman's technique

Undulating roof –outlined from the principles of regulated geometry– of the schools of the Sagrada Família

—vaulting *a la Catalan*— and is the direct precedent to shell vaulting so much used today by Candela, among others; to mention his incorporation of artisan skills into architecture, etc.; to even quote him as a formal source of the expressionism of Poelzig, Steiner and Mendelsohn all seems naïve compared to what has emerged from our passionate tale. The heresy of today's architecture is perhaps in only seeing certain "conditions" that are judged as strictly architectural, evaluating everything from a social or economic point of view, or from a technical one. Gaudí is the Michelangelo of a much more heartrending, complex and contradictory era than that of the 16th century. Not only is he the creator of a morphological universe applying the corresponding mechanical laws; he is also the absolute intellectual predecessor of the modern sculptural world and even the inspirer of a large part of "material" painting. However, far and above these artistic values, as well as the architectural values we have already mentioned, is the secret violence and sacred strength of his soul, shown in works that exist and are part of the history of mankind.

Original drawing by Gaudí that shows the Passion Façade of the Sagrada Família. It was produced in 1911 while he convalesced in Puigcerdà from brucellosis

▶ **Barcelona**

Heritage Site of National Interest
UNESCO World Heritage Site

Basilica of the
Sagrada Família

Construction work began on the Sagrada
Família in 1882. Its promoter, Josep Bocabella,
entrusted the work to the architect Francisco
de Paula del Villar who, in 1883, was replaced
by Gaudí. From this moment on, the work on
the temple would accompany him for the rest
of his life and he introduced architectural
solutions that he had tested and solved in
other projects. The temple, that would be
called the "Cathedral of the Poor", had to be
financed entirely by donations. The works
continue up to this day, following the plans
that the architect left behind.

▶ **Anagram**

The pinnacle of the
first pediment of the
cloister carries the
anagram of the Holy
Family. Beneath the
cross of Jesus, the saw
of Saint Joseph with
the M of Mary inter-
laced, in a design simi-
lar to that of the
mosaic of the vaulting
keystone in the crypt
of the Colònia Güell.

▶ ## Basilica of the Sagrada Família Sardenya and Marina. Barcelona

The church, of basilican plan and with a Latin cross, has five naves in the central part and three in the transept. The limited area of ground where it had to be constructed (a single block in the Eixample district) meant that Gaudí took the fullest advantage of the space, which is why he placed the cloister around the temple.

The current state of the works, still in the process of construction, gives one an idea of the massive proportions the building will have once it is completed. It will have very high bell towers, the highest one, symbolising Jesus, will be 170 m tall. Around it will be built four more, which will represent the Evangelists. Another will be erected over the apse and will be in dedication to the Virgin Mary whereas to the eight existing bell towers (the Nativity and Passion facades) will be added another four on the main facade (in dedication to the Glory), which will symbolise the twelve apostles.

The style of the Sagrada Família is Gothic-based from developing controlled geometric structures. The work combines the essence of Gaudí's knowledge and constructive experience, featuring the paraboloidal base structure, the generation of the columns in the central nave and its tree-shaped form that supports vaulting of a hyperbolic base, as well as the interior modulation of the side windows that filter and distribute the light.

In the north-east corner, Gaudí set up his workshop, where he had the site office, a study space and the storeroom for archive material. It was here where he built the large-scale models, experimenting with the geometry, colours, forms and sounds; he designed the liturgical furniture of the temple, preserved his entire project and even stayed up all night working during the last months of his life. In 1936 the workshop was burnt down and the greater part of the project was lost, something that did not stop the work being continued and which is being carried on today.

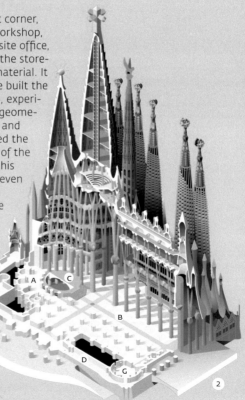

Construction 1882-1926

1 Nativity Façade
2 Glory Façade
3 Passion Façade

A Apse
B Central nave
C Altar
D Cloister
E Chapel of the Rosary
F Sacristy
G Baptistery
H Chapel of Penitence
I Schools

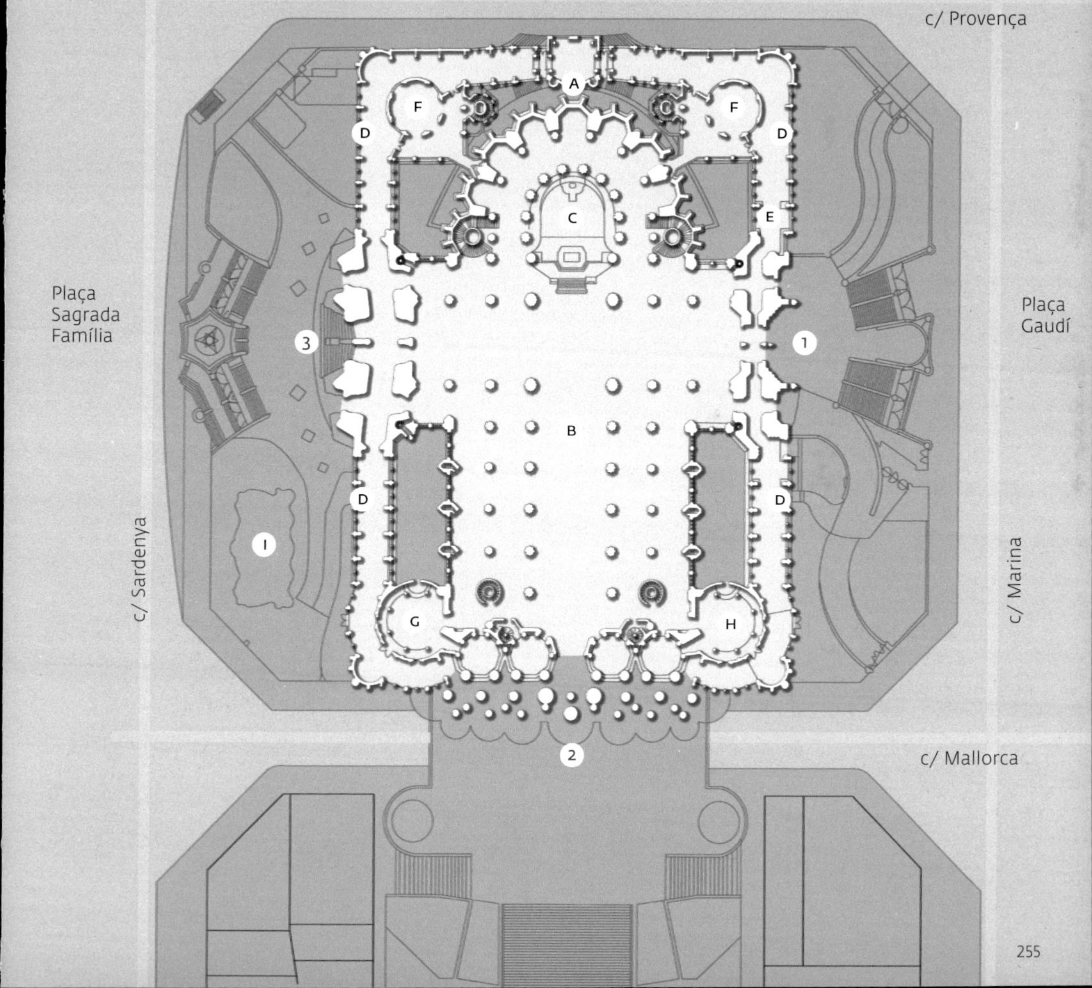
c/ Provença
Plaça Sagrada Família
Plaça Gaudí
c/ Sardenya
c/ Marina
c/ Mallorca
A
B
C
D
E
F
G
H
I
1
2
3

▶ # Basilica of the Sagrada Família

▸ Bishops

The towers of the three façades are dedicated to the twelve apostles, the first bishops of the church. For this reason they are crowned by pinnacles with the Episcopal symbols: the mitre, the crozier, the cross and the ring.

Hosanna Excelsis

Each letter inscribed in a hexagon, these words ("glory on high") are found at the base of the pinnacle and are sung at the end of the Sanctus, also written towards the centre of the tower.

▸ Original sketch

In 1906 a unique original drawing by Gaudí was published about the temple of the Sagrada Família that shows its volumes and towers once finalised.

▸ The Tau, the X and the dove

The anagram of the Holy Trinity crowns the cypress, the Tau – first letter of the name of God in Greek– of the Father, the cross in the form of crosspiece of the Son and the dove of the Holy Ghost.

Nativity

Over the column of the genealogy of Jesus –central column of the Nativity Façade and which divides the Charity Doorway in two– stands the sculptural group of the nativity. Joseph protects Mary and both adore the baby Jesus, with the ox and the mule from popular tradition on both sides.

Pelican

Symbol of the Eucharist, and therefore of the sacrifice of Jesus, in early Christianity, is found at the foot of the cypress, symbol of eternal life.

▶ Basilica of the Sagrada Família

◀ **Six toes**
In the sculptural group of the Slaughter of the Innocents, the foot of the soldier that is about to tear apart a child has six toes.

▶ **Musician angels**
Six angels, three with classical instruments and three with popular instruments, symbolise the celestial court of the Baby Jesus.

◀ **Birds**
It seems as if they are coming out of the stone flying in all directions and are the symbol of the relationship between heaven and earth, divine messengers against the serpent.

▶ **Temptation**
In the chapel of the Rosary, a demonic being places an Orsini bomb –used in the attack on the Liceu theatre in 1893– in the hands of a worker.

Angel of the Final Judgement

The figures on the Nativity Façade were made from moulds of people. In this case the illustrator Opisso, assistant to Gaudí.

Roman soldiers

With helmets that imitate the chimneys of the Pedrera, they are homage to Gaudí by the sculptor Subirachs.

Carpenter's tools

In the Hope Doorway there are many tools related to the construction trade.

The Veronica

The face of Jesus printed on the veil of the Veronica always looks at the spectator through an optical effect produced by the sculptor Subirachs.

→
IN 1892 GAUDÍ BEGAN THE
NATIVITY FACADE.
ON THE 30TH OF NOVEMBER
1925 THE FIRST BELL TOWER,
DEDICATED TO ST. BARNABUS,
WAS COMPLETED. GAUDÍ SPOKE
OF HIS PLEASURE OF SEEING
"HOW THAT SPEAR JOINS
HEAVEN AND EARTH".
→
COMPUTER GRAPHIC
RECONSTRUCTION OF THE
APPEARANCE THE TEMPLE WILL
HAVE ONCE THE WORKS HAVE
BEEN COMPLETED.

P. 262-263
→
THE TRUMPETER ANGELS BY
THE SCULPTOR LLORENÇ
MATAMALA WERE PLACED
IN 1899.
→
THE FOUR BELL TOWERS ON
THE FACADE OF THE NATIVITY
WERE COMPLETED IN 1930.

→
SNAIL ON ONE OF THE APSE
CORNERS.

→
THE DIZZY SPIRAL OF THE STEPS
ON THE INSIDE OF THE TOWERS
IS FASCINATING AS IT TAKES US
INTO THE INSIDE OF A GIGANTIC
STONE SNAIL.

P. 266-267
→
THE TORTOISE, A SYMBOLIC
ANIMAL OVER WHICH THE
UNIVERSE IS SUPPORTED, IS AT
THE FOOT OF THE COLUMNS
OF THE FACADE OF THE
NATIVITY.

→
REPRESENTATION OF THE
ZODIACAL SIGN OF TAURUS.

→
OVER THE GROUND PLAN THAT
WAS STARTED BY FRANCISCO
DE PAULA DEL VILLAR, GAUDÍ
COMPLETED THE CRYPT.

→
VAULTING KEYSTONE IN
THE CRYPT WITH THE
REPRESENTATION OF THE
ANNUNCIATION OF MARY
BY THE SCULPTOR FLOTATS.

→
IN 1899 THE CHAPEL IN THE
CLOISTER OF THE VIRGIN OF
THE ROSARY WAS COMPLETED
AND ON WHICH GAUDÍ
WORKED WITH EXTREME
EXACTITUDE ON THE DETAILS.

→
DETAIL OF THE DOORS OF THE
NATIVITY FAÇADE PRODUCED BY
ETSURO SOTOO.

→
IN 1911 GAUDÍ BECAME ILL WITH MALTESE FEVER AND FROM HIS CONVALESCENCE IN PUIGCERDÀ HE IMAGINED THE FACADE OF THE PASSION: "I AM PREPARED TO SACRIFICE THE VERY CONSTRUCTION, TO BREAK VAULTING AND CUT COLUMNS TO GIVE AN IDEA OF HOW CRUEL SACRIFICE IS".

→
IN 1990, IN THE ATRIUM OF THE FACADE OF THE PASSION, THE FIRST SCULPTURES ENTRUSTED TO JOSEP MARIA SUBIRACHS WERE POSITIONED.

→

THE 40-METRE-HIGH WESTERN
SACRISTY IS THE ONLY ONE OF
THE TWO GAUDÍ DESIGNED
THAT HAS BEEN COMPLETED.
AFTER THE DESTRUCTION OF
GAUDÍ'S MODELS DURING THE
CIVIL WAR, THE
RECONSTRUCTION OF THE
SACRISTY ALLOWED US TO SEE
THAT THE DOME WAS FORMED
WITH AN INTERSECTION OF
12 PARABOLOIDS JOINED IN THE
UPPER VERTEX. THIS FORM IS
HIGHLY RESISTANT AND IS
WHAT GAUDÍ ALSO PROPOSED
FOR THE CENTRAL TOWERS.

→

VIEW FROM THE APSE IN ITS
CURRENT STATE. IN THE
CENTRE, NOW VISIBLE, IS THE
TOWER DEDICATED TO THE
VIRGIN, WHICH WILL BE
CROWNED BY A LUMINOUS
STAR, THE *STELLA MATUTINA*.
THIS TOWER, LOCATED ABOVE
THE CRYPT, AT 140 M, WILL BE
THE HIGHEST AFTER THAT OF
JESUS.

→
ALONG WITH THE VAULTS, THE
STAINED-GLASS WINDOWS
FILTER THE LIGHT JUST AS
GAUDÍ HAD WISHED,
SIMULATING THE LIGHTING THE
INTERIOR OF A FOREST
RECEIVES THROUGH THE
LEAVES OF THE TREES.

P. 278-279
→→
THE NAVE REPRODUCES THE
IDEA OF THE FOREST OF
COLUMNS, SOME OF WHICH
REACH 21 METRES IN HEIGHT AS
THE TREES BRANCH OFF ON
REACHING THE VAULTING.

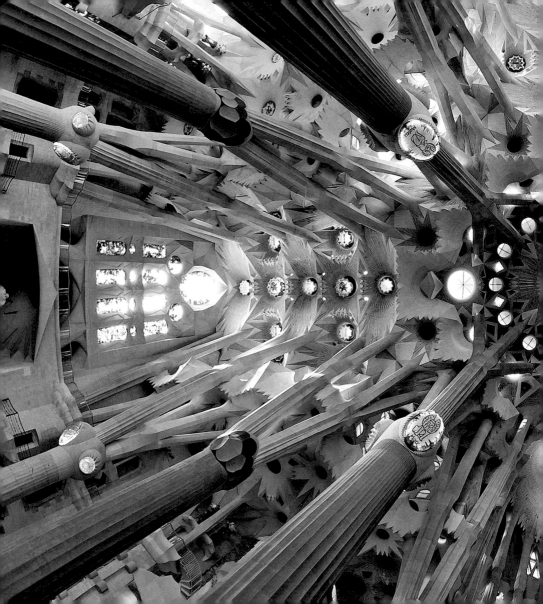

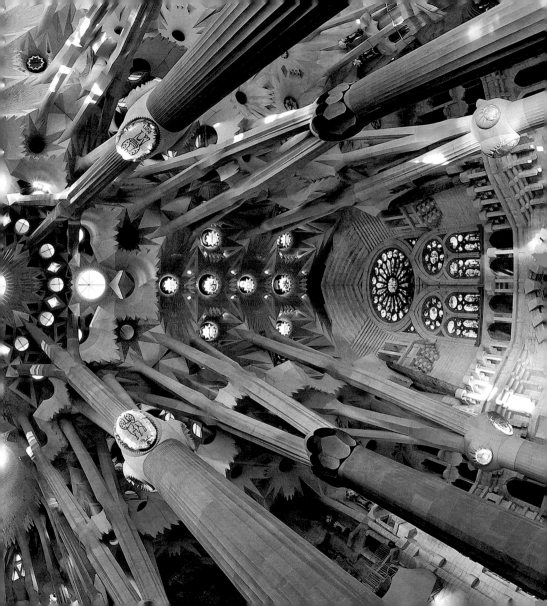

Antoni Gaudí (1852–1926)

1852 Antoni Gaudí was born in Reus.

1867 With Eduard Toda and Josep Ribera, he conceives a restoration plan for the monastery of Poblet.

1869 He moves to Barcelona with his brother Francesc.

1872 He enrols at the Higher School of Architecture of Barcelona.

1876 The deaths of his brother, Francesc, and his mother have a profound effect on the young Gaudí's state of mind and he seeks refuge in his architectural studies. From this period are preserved projects such as the cemetery gate or the jetty. To pay for his studies, Gaudí worked with two recognised professionals in Barcelona: Francesc de Paula del Villar and Josep Fontserè i Mestre, who he helped in Ciutadella Park where he produced, among other pieces, the two naturalist panels at the Aquarium entrance, which is behind the monumental waterfall.

1877 He finishes the graduate project for a university auditorium.

1878 He creates a display cabinet for the Comella glove shop, exhibited at the Universal Exhibition of Paris. He completes his studies at the School of Architecture. The principal, Elies Rogent, states, "I don't know whether we have given the qualification to a madman or a genius".He designs the Girossi news stand and lampposts for Barcelona City Council. After seeing the Comella display cabinet, Eusebi Güell takes an interest in Gaudí's work and commissions him with the liturgical furniture for the chapel of Antonio López in Comillas.He undertakes several projects for the Mataró Cooperative Society of which the watercolour that was shown at the Universal Exhibition of Paris still survives.

1879 Gaudí's sister dies and he takes over the guardianship of his niece Rosa Egea. He decorates the Gibert pharmacy and joins the Catalan Association for Scientific Excursions.

1881 He publishes an article in the magazine *La Renaixença*. He builds a news stand to commemorate the visit of King Alfons XII to Comillas.

1882 He draws up the project of Joan Martorell who took part in a bid for the facade of the cathedral of Barcelona and designs a hunting lodge for the property of Eusebi Güell in Garraf. Neither project is ever realised.

1883 Proposed by Joan Martorell, Gaudí replaces F. de P. del Villar as head of the works of the Sagrada Família. He begins work on the Casa Vicens and El Capricho in Comillas. As his assistant, he employs a young man aged 17, Francesc Berenguer. He uses the catenary arch for the first time in the bleaching room of the Mataró Cooperative.

1884 He signs the first official document as architect of the Sagrada Família. He begins the pavilions of the Güell estate in Les Corts.

1885 First full project for the Sagrada Família. He designs the Dragon Gateway of the Güell Pavilions.

1886 After producing several design variations of the Palau Güell facade, Gaudí, helped by Berenguer, comes up with a solution that he presents

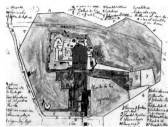
1867 Project for restoration of Poblet

1876 Project for jetty

1877 Project for university auditorium

1878 Mataronense Cooperative Company

1881 Newsstand in Comillas

1882 Project for hunting lodge in Garraf

1883 Crypt of the Temple of the Sagrada Família

1885 Pavilions of the Güell estate

1886 Palau Güell

to Barcelona City Council. He begins construction work of the Palau Güell.

1887 With Domènech i Montaner he travels to Manises (Valencia) in order to learn the traditional techniques of glazed pottery. He finishes the pavilions of the Güell estate.

1888 He makes the pavilion for the Compañia Transatlántica in the Universal exhibition of Barcelona. He makes a project for the decoration –unrealised– of the Saló de Cent (Council Chamber). He completes the Casa Vicens and Enric d'Ossó commissions him with the work for the Theresan College.

1890 The trips to León and Astorga begin. Joan Baptista Grau, the bishop of Astorga, has a profound influence on Gaudí's religious thinking. He finishes the Theresan College.

1891 Gaudí signs the project for the Casa Botines in León.

1892 He builds the Casa Botines in ten months. He starts the project for the Nativity Façade. The apse of the Sagrada Família reaches a height of 20 metres.

1893 He abandons the work on the Episcopal Palace of Astorga without finishing the roofing. He undertakes the project for the Franciscan Catholic Missions of Tangier in Africa which, while never being realised, shows a similarity to the

temple of the Sagrada Família. He finishes the apse of the temple.

1894 The foundations of the Nativity Façade are completed and its construction begins. A Lent fast puts the architect's life at risk. Bishop Torras i Bages persuades him to abandon the penitence.

1895 He plans the Güell Bodegas in Garraf.

1898 He presents the project for the Casa Calvet. He begins the studies for the construction of the church of the Güell Industrial Village and the development of the polyfunicular model.

1899 He joins two Catalan institutions with a catholic ideology: The Artistic Circle of Sant Lluc and the Spiritual league of the Virgin of Montserrat, which commissions Gaudí to build the First Mystery of Glory.

1900 He starts work on Bellesguard and Park Güell. He completes the Casa Calvet, which receives the prize from the City Council for the best building in Barcelona. Some sculptures are placed on the Nativity Façade. Donations for the temple run short.

1902 He builds the doorway for the estate of H. Miralles and takes part in the decoration of the Café Torino (no longer in existence).

1888 Casa Vicens

1890 Theresan College

1891 Casa Botines

1893 Episcopal Palace of Astorga

1893 Apse of the Temple of the Sagrada Família

1895 Güell Bodegas

1898 Polyfunicular model of the church of Güell industrial Village

1900 Casa Calvet

1902 Café Torino

1904 He embarks on the reform of the Cathedral of Mallorca and of the Casa Batlló for which he draws up a draft project that differs greatly from the final result. At the behest of Lluís Graner, he decorates the Sala Mercè, one of the first cinemas in Barcelona. Project that was never realised, also by Lluís Graner, for a chalet in the Bonanova district.

1905 He produces the Catllaràs chalet and the gardens of Can Artigues in La Pobla de Lillet.

1906 An original sketch by Gaudí of the Temple of the complete Sagrada Família is published. He moves, with his father and niece, to the house in Park Güell built by Berenguer. His father dies on the 29th of October. Construction work begins on the Casa Milà, "La Pedrera".

1907 He finishes the Casa Batlló.

1908 After ten years of studies, work starts on the church of Güell Industrial Village. According to Joan Matamala, Gaudí received the commission from the North Americans to build a hotel in New York. Matamala reproduced the project in a drawing.

1909 He builds and self-finances the schools for the Temple of the Sagrada Família. He finishes his work on Bellesgard and leaves his collaborator Sugrañes to finish off some details.

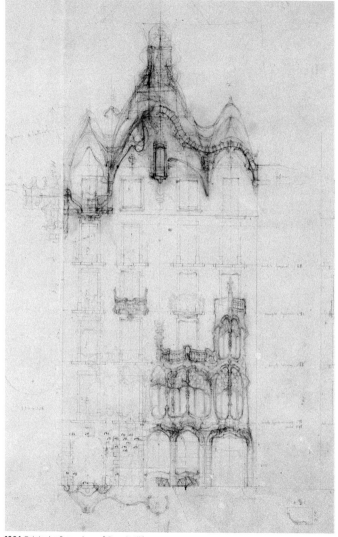

1904 Original reform plans of Casa Batlló

1910 A polychrome model of the Nativity Façade is exhibited in Paris. Gaudí rests in Vic to recover from anaemia and designs, together with Jujol and Canaleta, some lampposts for the town's main square and which would disappear in 1924.

1911 Gaudí falls ill with brucellosis and is taken to Puigcerdà to recover. While there, he plans the Passion Façade.

1912 His niece, Rosa Egea, dies. He finishes the Casa Milà.

1913 The undulating bench in Park Güell is completed on which the collaboration of Jujol is evident.

1914 He finishes the work on Park Güell. Work is halted on the church of the Güell industrial Village. His friend and collaborator F. Berenguer dies. Gaudí devotes his time to the Sagrada Família.

1915 He undertakes a rehearsal with tubular bells in the towers of the Sagrada Família.

1916 The lack of donations to build the Sagrada Família forces Gaudí to make street collections. This circumstance is both satirised and politicised by the republican press of the time which publishes a cartoon strip in which Güell heads a procession of outstanding figures who beg for charity with the temple in the background.

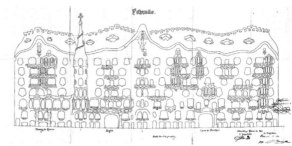

1906 Project for Casa Milà "La Pedrera"

1907 Casa Batlló

1908 Crypt of Güell industrial Village

1909 Schools of the Temple of the Sagrada Família

1909 Bellesguard Tower

1910 Lampposts for the main square of Vic

1918 Eusebi Güell Bacigalupi dies.

1923 Definitive solution for the naves and roofing in 1:10 and 1:25 scale plaster models. The central bell towers of the Nativity Façade reach a height of eighty metres.

1924 On the eleventh of September Gaudí is arrested when he goes to a mass held in honour of the Catalans who fell in defence of Barcelona in 1714.

1925 The tower of St. Barnabus is completed on the 30th of November with the pinnacle. Gaudí exclaims his joy, "on seeing how that lance joins the heavens with the earth". Gaudí moves to the Sagrada Família workshops.

1926 Gaudí dies after being run over by a tram. The streets of Barcelona are filled with people who accompany the funeral procession. The architect was buried in the crypt of the Sagrada Família.

1925 Gaudí's bedroom

1925 Gaudí's studio in the Sagrada Família

1918 Eusebi Güell Bacigalupi

1925 Temple of the Sagrada Família

1926 Gaudí's funeral

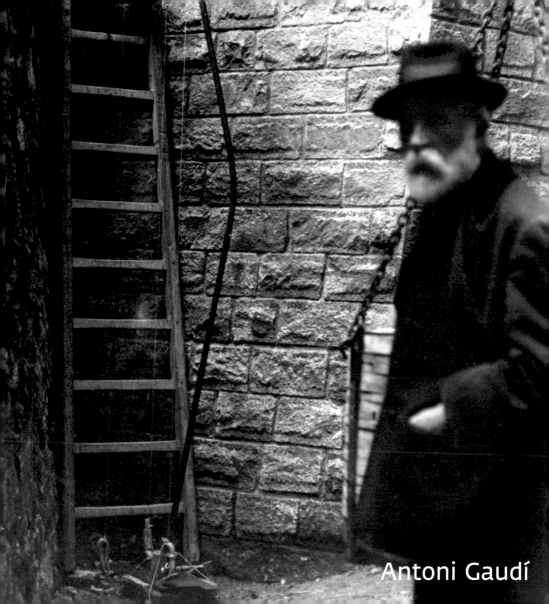

Antoni Gaudí

GAUDÍ
Introduction to his architecture

© Triangle Postals

© Original text:
Lourdes and Victoria Cirlot

© Photography:
Pere Vivas, Ricard Pla
Casa Batlló, pages 180, 186, 187, 188, 190, 191, 192, 193,
194, 195, 196, 197, 198, 199, 200, 201, 202, 203, 204, 205
Pere Vivas / Basílica de la Sagrada Família,
pages 13, 265, 268, 269, 270, 276, 278
Biel Puig, page 188, 198, 199
Jordi Puig / Pere Vivas, pages 170, 174, 175
Juanjo Puente / Pere Vivas, pages 146
Rafael Vargas, pages 126, 133
Jordi Puig, page 245b

Archive photographs:
Arxiu Gràfic de la Càtedra Gaudí
Arxiu Històric de la Ciutat de Barcelona
Junta Constructora del Temple de la Sagrada Família
Museu Comarcal Salvador Vilaseca. Reus
Col·lecció privada Antoni González Moreno-Navarro, page 245a
Col·lecció privada Juan-José Lahuerta, page 152

Complementary texts:
Antonio G. Funes, Josep Liz

Translation:
Steve Cedar

Plans:
CAIRAT, UPC, Joan Font, David Martínez

Design:
Joan Colomer

Layout:
Oleguer Farriol, Aina Pla, Genís Puig

Registration number:
B. 31363-2010

ISBN:
978-84-8478-451-7

Printed in Barcelona 3-2018

Acknowledgements:
Ajuntament de Mataró
Capítol de la Catedral de Mallorca
Casa Batlló
Casa-Museu Gaudí
Casa Vicens Gaudí
Col·legi de les Teresianes
Consorci de la Colònia Güell
Fundació Catalunya La Pedrera
Institut Municipal de Parcs i Jardins,
Ajuntament de Barcelona
Junta Constructora del Temple Expiatori
de la Sagrada Família
Museu d'Història de Barcelona
Obispado de Astorga
Palau Güell
Càtedra Gaudí
Restaurant Casa Calvet
Restaurant Gaudí Garraf
Torre Bellesguard Gaudí. Família Guilera
Daniel Giralt-Miracle
Juan-José Lahuerta

TRIANGLE ▾ BOOKS